MAKING AND DRESSING
TRADITIONAL
TEDDY BEARS

BRIAN & DONNA GIBBS

David & Charles

A DAVID & CHARLES BOOK

First published in the UK in 2000

Text, illustrations and designs Copyright © Brian and Donna Gibbs 2000
Photography and layout Copyright © David & Charles 2000

Brian and Donna Gibbs have asserted their right to be identified as authors of this work in
accordance with the Copyright, Designs and Patents Act, 1988.

A catalogue record for this book is available from the British Library.

ISBN 0 7153 0796 7
Photography by Jon Stewart
Styling by Barbara Stewart
Step-by-step photography by David Johnson
Book design by Margaret Foster
Edited by Juliet Bracken

Printed in Italy by Milanostampa SpA
for David & Charles
Brunel House   Newton Abbot   Devon

CONTENTS

INTRODUCTION

Like our first book, *Making Traditional Teddy Bears*, this new book guides you step by step through the techniques of making and dressing a traditional teddy bear to treasure. These bears are designed in the style of the first bears made at the beginning of the twentieth century with long limbs and humped backs and using the same materials – mohair fabric, wooden joints, glass eyes and wood wool. They can be tackled successfully by beginners and experts alike. They are also shown dressed in a variety of outfits and styles to suit all tastes. Clear colour photographs and detailed line drawings will help you every step of the way to create a dressed teddy bear to be really proud of.

There is much lively debate among bear lovers as to whether or not traditional teddy bears should be dressed. Some believe that the beautiful mohair fabrics they are made from should remain uncovered, leaving the teddy bear to be appreciated as it is. Others will allow only a smart, colourful ribbon to adorn their favourite bear. All of the bear designs in this book can be made without clothes. Many others, however, will benefit from the extra character that a teddy takes on when they are dressed in a range of different outfits. The designs in this book will hopefully inspire those who want to create their own individual little characters in this way.

Throughout the book you will find advice on choosing the right fabrics and materials to make both the bears and their clothes, and a guide to the tools and components needed. You will also be introduced to such delightful characters as Georgie (see page 30), an eight-inch mascot bear who has a mix and match wardrobe made from a few simple pattern pieces, and the brother and sister bears Hugo and Poppy (see page 38), who are both dressed for a day in the countryside. Then there's Grandpa Harry and Grandma Harriet (see page 46), who are shown sitting in comfortable rocking chairs wearing spectacles and slippers, and Mei Ying and Mei Yang (see page 52), two oriental characters. Finally, the beautiful and elaborate Anastasia (see page 58), a bear of royal grandeur who stands 18 inches tall, is the princess with a sumptuous satin ballgown and lined velvet cloak. For colder winter days she has a lined fur coat with matching hat and muff to keep out the winter chill.

All the procedures are clearly explained with photographs and diagrams, so you can confidently tackle any of the projects. At the end of the book there is a short section on adapting the patterns to suit a differently-sized teddy bear. We hope this will also encourage you to be creative and change the outfits to make your bear unique. Finally, you will find a list of suppliers and bear-related contact addresses at the back of the book to help you obtain the high quality materials you need.

Instructions for making this cosy outfit for
Anastasia are found on page 61.

MAKING THE BEARS

I n this chapter you will find a brief guide to the fabrics, joints, eyes and other materials you will need to make a traditional teddy bear. Details are also included on the tools and other equipment required. Once you have put together these items, you will be ready to make your bear using our comprehensive step-by-step guide on page 13. Whether you are a complete beginner or an experienced bear-maker, you will enjoy working through the various stages illustrated by colour photographs or diagrams.

MATERIALS & EQUIPMENT

At one time home bear-makers could only buy synthetic fur fabrics, but now natural fabrics such as mohair and alpaca are available by mail order from specialist suppliers. With some companies offering up to a thousand fabrics, you may find choosing one a little daunting. To help you, we have specified the exact fabric used for the bears in this book. You can either recreate the same look or try a different pile length or finish to create your own unique bear.

MOHAIR

Mohair fabric has to be the preferred choice for making a traditional teddy bear. It was used to make the first teddy bears at the beginning of the twentieth century and is now available in a bewildering range of styles and pile lengths. Although it may seem quite expensive, using mohair will give your teddy bear a silky feel and ensure it lasts a lifetime.

Mohair fabric is made from a natural fibre taken from the fleece of an angora goat. This is woven onto a cotton backing, usually in enormous 30-metre lengths. Mohair lends itself really well to traditional teddy bear making because the cotton backing does not stretch out of shape when the bear is stuffed. This is important because traditional bears are usually firmly stuffed.

Mohair is available in a large range of pile lengths, colours and finishes. The main types are given here. The pile length can vary from 4mm to over 25mm, and the longer piles come in different finishes, too. Generally, the shortest pile fabrics are the cheapest and the best suited to making small bears.

STRAIGHT PILE

Straight-pile mohair is the basic mohair which receives no extra treatment after it has been woven. It is available in all pile lengths and is often described as the easiest mohair to use. Since all of the pile lies in the same direction on this fabric, the pattern can be laid onto the fabric following the pile direction with no further checking needed. Most short-pile mohair fabrics are only available as straight pile.

DISTRESSED PILE

Distressed-pile mohair is treated to give the fabric an aged look. This finish is applied with a machine first used for crushing velvet that compacts the fabric. The mohair is passed through the machine still wet from dyeing. Once dry, it is stretched back into shape and set with heat to form a pile that faces different ways. Your bear will look as if it has had years of cuddling.

SPARSE PILE

The density of a mohair fabric is determined by the number of threads used per inch to weave it. Sparse mohair has relatively few threads per inch which makes the cotton backing fabric clearly visible through the pile. This is ideal for creating a bear that looks even older than one made from distressed mohair. The fur on a bear made from sparse-pile fabric can look as if it is wearing away – just like many of the collectible bears sold at auction.

The low density of the pile makes this fabric suitable for making small bears, as you can use a longer pile.

CURLY AND WAVE PILE

These finishes are usually found on long-pile fabrics. The long pile is given a uniform curl or wave which adds texture and interest to the fur. Wave finishes often form patterns such as 'A' and 'V' waves. Use this mohair to make large, magnificent bears such as Anastasia (see page 58), where the luxurious effect is more important than the cost of the fabric.

TIPPED PILE

Here the ends of the pile are tinted in a different colour to the rest. This can give your bear a very realistic appearance when natural colours are used, and it is also available in more outrageous colourings, too. The colour on the tips can be either darker or lighter than the pile underneath. Stunning effects can be created – usually on the face – by trimming off the top colour to allow the main colour to show through.

LOOM STATE

Mohair can be used when it comes off the weaving looms without any finishes or dyes being applied to it. It is available in its natural cream colouring and the pile looks and feels like no other mohair. Use it to make a truly individual bear or, if you want a special colour that you cannot find in the specialist suppliers' catalogues, for home dyeing. This is easy to do, although you will loose the unique texture of this fur in the process.

The choice does not end there. Mohair is manufactured in various countries and specialist suppliers will often import fabrics if required. English mohair, for example, is woven in Yorkshire. It has a silky texture but also a very natural feel. It is woven onto a firm cotton fabric and is extremely durable. By contrast, the pile on German mohair has a different feel. It is a luxurious pile woven onto a soft backing. This can be helpful when turning the bear the right way out after stitching. But if you are making a small bear you may need to use a fixative on the cut edges before sewing to stop the fabric from fraying.

South African mohair is a more recent addition to this market. This has such a dense pile that you cannot see the woven backing. The pile is beautifully soft and can be made to look different by brushing the bear. This gives the pile a wispy effect. The backing fabric can be quite thick and may fray, so this wonderful fabric is not recommended for making your first bear.

Home bear-makers are spoilt for choice when it comes to choosing the fabric to make their bear from. There are hundreds of types of mohair and many excellent synthetic fur fabrics, too.

OTHER BEAR-MAKING FABRICS

MOHAIR AND WOOL MIX

This mix of fibres woven onto a cotton backing is less expensive than pure mohair. Although the pile of this fabric does not have the silky feel of mohair, it still has a soft texture and will make up into a perfectly acceptable traditional teddy bear. This may be a good choice when making a bear for a child.

ALPACA

This is another natural fabric similar to mohair. The pile, which is obtained from a type of llama instead of a goat, is very soft and dense, and holds its natural texture. The pile may have small variations in colour and this can be used to great effect to create more natural-looking bears.

SYNTHETIC FUR FABRIC

In the 1950s teddy bears began to be made from washable synthetic fur fabrics instead of mohair. Until fairly recently, when suppliers began to stock such a wide range of mohair, the home bear-maker could only buy synthetic fur fabrics to create their bears. These can be used to make a traditional teddy bear but will not give quite the same look as mohair.

The best-quality synthetic fur fabrics are made with a woven backing to ensure that a bear holds its shape when it is stuffed. They are quite expensive but should still only be about half the price of the equivalent mohair fabric. They come in a large range of colours and pile lengths, but the pile may be susceptible to matting when handled. They are usually only available through specialist bear- or toy-making suppliers (see page 127).

The cheaper fur fabrics you will find in craft shops or markets have a knitted jersey backing. These are not suitable for making traditional teddy bears because the backing easily stretches out of shape at the stuffing stage, with the result that the finished bear does not look like the pattern at all. The pile on the cheapest fur fabrics can matt very easily and is usually much thinner than the more expensive synthetic furs. However, the cheaper fabrics are perfectly adequate for making softly-stuffed children's toys. You could also use these fabrics for a first attempt at bear-making. Prepare the fabric by fixing some very firm iron-on interfacing to the backing. This will prevent the backing from stretching out of shape and ensure that your finished bear looks something like the original.

MINI-BEAR FABRICS

Making miniature bears (less than 8cm (3in) high) has its own dedicated following, too (see Bedtime Georgie on page 31). It's not hard to master the art of making bears on this scale, but for the best results you need to use smaller-scale fabrics. You can use the shortest pile mohair fabric to make a bear of 8cm (3in), but the weight and firmness of the backing fabric will make turning the pieces after sewing difficult. Miniature bear artists now have a whole range of upholstery fabrics to choose from. These distinctive materials have a special backing that does not fray or need to be fixed, and they are more pliable than mohair or synthetic fur fabrics. They are available in most colours including animal prints. Specialist miniature-bear-making suppliers (see page 127) stock a good range of these reasonably-priced fabrics.

OTHER SUITABLE FABRICS

Just about any woven material can be used to make teddy bears. Over the years, they have been made from many fabrics including printed cottons, patchwork, blankets and even hessian sacking. If you choose a material with no pile, pick a design that is roundly proportioned instead of one with long thin limbs. If the fabric is a little plain, add some embroidery to create more interest on the finished bear.

PAD MATERIALS

Teddy bear paws and pads are usually made from felt, leather, suede, or ultra-suede. Traditionally, teddy bears were given felt pads, which were often replaced with other fabrics when the felt wore out. This explains why many old teddies have materials other than felt stitched to their feet.

FELT

This versatile material is available in many different shades, and is extremely easy to cut and sew. It is made by milling wet fibres until they matt and then applying pressure to set them. This method ensures that the finished felt has no grain line and pieces can be cut out from it very economically. Like most fabrics felt is available in different qualities.

The cheapest felt is made from acrylic fibres and tends to be very thin. This should be used as a double layer for bear-making: cut out two of each paw and foot pad piece and tack (baste) them together before making up your bear. Next in quality is a mix of acrylic and wool fibres, (usually 60% wool to 40% synthetic). The wool fibres in this material make it thicker and more durable, but the cost is still very reasonable. The best-quality felt is made from 100% wool fibres. This is very thick, has a finer texture than cheaper felt and is extremely hard wearing.

LEATHER AND SUEDE

Natural materials such as leather and suede look very effective when used for paws and pads but are very difficult to sew. The leather gives naturally by stretching in all directions making it hard to sew by machine. Sewing by hand is no better as the toughness of the leather makes special needles necessary. If you are really keen to use leather, buy the thinner type used in clothing.

ULTRA-SUEDE

This man-made fabric is very easy to work with and is available in a wide variety of colours from specialist bear-making suppliers. It has a short velvety pile and a woven backing that does not fray when cut out. It is also available in a distressed-pile finish, which can be made into very effective miniature bears.

THREADS

SEWING MACHINE THREAD

You will need sewing thread to sew your bear together. If you are using a sewing machine you will need good-quality cotton or polyester/cotton sewing thread. Either of these types of thread is suitable, but polyester/cotton may be slightly stronger. However, this does not really matter since the seams should be stitched twice when using a machine. Match the thread to the colour of the backing on your fabric. When you lay a single thread across the back it should be barely visible. This will ensure your stitches are not noticeable.

EXTRA-STRONG THREAD

This much thicker, heavy-duty thread is used to finish the seams left open for turning and stuffing, and for attaching glass eyes. In both of these tasks the thread has to be pulled very tightly so it is essential that it is strong enough to take the strain. Test the thread by trying to break a short section with your hands. If you are sewing your bear by hand, this extra-strong thread should be used for every stage of the stitching.

NOSE THREAD

Experienced teddy bear makers often try using different threads to sew the nose on their bears, but traditionally it should be cotton. Perle cotton, used in embroidery, is perfect for creating the noses on teddy bears. It is available in an assortment of shades and

also in two weights. The lighter one is particularly suitable for miniature teddy bears. Black and brown are the shades most commonly used, but highly distinctive bears can be created by using other colours.

FILLINGS

There are a few points to bear in mind before choosing the type of filling to use for your bear. If the bear is intended for a child, make certain that the filling and all the other components used comply with the relevant safety standards. If you want your teddy bear to be as traditional as possible, consider using old-fashioned materials such as wood wool and kapok. To give your bear more character it is possible to buy fillings that create a saggy old look.

POLYESTER

This is the easiest and cleanest filling to use and is the only choice for children's bears. The better quality hi-loft varieties make the task of stuffing a teddy bear much easier because they are unlikely to knot up or compress so much that lumps and bumps are formed. Cheaper varieties are available but you may need more filling and a little more patience.

KAPOK

Although it still features in the upholstery trade, kapok is not generally used any more for making teddy bears. It is a natural vegetable fibre with a silky feel made of very fine fibres that have a tendency to float about. These fibres may be a hazard to some people and a dust mask should be worn when using large quantities of kapok to prevent them from being inhaled. It is ideal for stuffing miniature bears because it is not as dense as the polyester fillings and so can be compressed to fill the small areas in a miniature bear.

WOOD WOOL

Traditionally, teddy bears were filled with wood wool, sold under the trade name Excelsior. This is very fine shredded wood that looks rather like straw. It is not suitable for children's bears because it is not washable and may have a high dust content. But if you want to make a truly traditional bear, this is the best filling to use. Filling a bear with wood wool takes time because it needs to be packed in very firmly, especially in the nose area, to create a firm platform ready for embroidering. Mix wood wool with polyester in the paw and foot pads to create soft and rounded feet and paws. This will also stop sharp pieces of wood wool from poking through the soft pad material.

PELLETS

These are a modern addition to bear-making materials and are often used together with other soft fillings such as polyester. They can give a bear a lot of character by making him look as though his filling has collapsed over the years and has fallen in a heap at the bottom of his tummy. The pellets are made from a range of different materials and some are heavier than others. Plastic pellets are the lightest of all. These are little balls of plastic used in large bears to prevent them from being too heavy. You can also buy pellets made from steel shot. These are much finer and heavier than the plastic versions and are better suited to small bears.

Glass pellets are the finest of all. Suited to miniature bears, these pellets will give the tiniest of bears a satisfying heaviness. Never use lead shot (even for collector's bears) because of the risk of lead poisoning, especially if you tend to cuddle your bears a lot.

JOINTS

All traditional teddy bears were jointed so that the arms, legs and head could move. Different methods of jointing have been tried over the years but now joints are made from wooden or plastic discs.

WOODEN JOINTS

A typical traditional joint used to attach a limb or head to the body is made up of two wooden discs, two metal washers and a split pin or cotter pin which is turned down with pliers to rest on the metal washer. To assemble, a metal washer is threaded onto the split pin followed by a wooden disc. This half joint is inserted into the limb or head and used to attach it to the body. A wooden disc and a metal washer are threaded onto the split pin to secure it from the inside and the split pin turned down.

MINIATURE JOINTS

Miniature joints are available in incredibly small sizes so that even the tiniest teddy bear can be jointed. Smaller joints are often made from thin fibreboard, and supplied without the metal washers due to their small size.

NUT AND BOLT JOINTS

You can also buy wooden joints that have a bolt instead of a split pin and are fixed with a Nylock nut. You may prefer this type of joint if you find using pliers difficult. Nut and bolt joints are attached by holding the head of the bolt with a spanner while the nut is tightened. The limbs are attached to the body before they are stuffed, but the head needs to be stuffed before it is attached. A Nylock nut cannot be used here because you won't be able to hold the bolt to tighten the nut. The best way to get round this problem is to replace the Nylock nut with two ordinary nuts. The first nut is tightened whilst holding the bolt from the inside of the body, then the second nut is tightened up to the first. This will hold the head firmly in place.

PLASTIC SAFETY JOINTS

Plastic joints are especially suitable for children's bears. They consist of two plastic discs and a star washer. One of the plastic discs has a moulded shank attached to it. This goes inside the limb and passes through the fabric to the outside in the same way as the split pin on a wooden joint. The limb is attached to the body and the second plastic disc is placed over the shank from the inside of the body and held in place with the metal washer. The only drawback with this type of joint is that once it has been fixed in place it cannot be removed without destroying the star washer.

EYES

BOOT-BUTTON EYES

Traditionally, bear manufacturers used actual boot buttons for the eyes on their teddies as no eyes were produced commercially at the time. It is possible to track down genuine antique boot buttons but you can also buy modern reproductions from specialist suppliers (see page 127). These are attached in the same way as glass eyes.

GLASS EYES

In 1909 manufacturers began producing teddy bear eyes made from glass in a wide range of colours and sizes. Today there is still a vast range of styles to choose from, and all eyes come with one of two types of fixing. The eyes either have a wire loop moulded into the back of each one (these are generally of better quality), or they are sold in pairs with the two eyes joined together by a piece of wire. This wire then has to be cut in the centre and twisted to form a loop on each eye. The main drawback with these is that the two eyes that make up a pair often do not match.

PLASTIC SAFETY EYES

These are the only eyes you should use on children's teddies. They are easily obtained from craft shops and are available in many different colours and sizes. They have to be fixed in place before the head is stuffed and are secured with a star washer. This washer can only be removed by cutting it off once it has been fixed. It is a good idea to mark the eye positions on your pattern and transfer them to the back of the fabric before you start sewing, to ensure that the eyes are level on your finished bear.

MINIATURE-BEAR EYES

Use either glass eyes with loops or beads on miniature bears. You can buy 2mm glass eyes which will be suitable for most miniature bears. Glass or plastic beads with a hole in the centre can also be used.

VOICES

Traditional teddy bears were often given voices to make them growl. Growlers come in various sizes so you need to check that it will fit inside your bear's tummy. If the bear is too small for a growler, one alternative is a small plastic squeaker, although these may be more suited to children's toys. It is also possible to make your bear melodious by adding a musical movement. There are many different ones you can buy, but you must pick a movement that is sealed inside a plastic shell.

ESSENTIAL TOOLS

Making a traditional teddy bear is a fairly straight-forward process that does not need a lot of specialist equipment. In fact, most of the tools needed can usually be found around the home. You can buy any tools you need from specialist teddy-bear-making suppliers (see page 127). Good-quality tools are essential as these will make the job much easier and will not let you down at a crucial stage.

Whether you sew your bear by hand or by machine is a matter of personal preference. Very large bears often take much longer if sewn by hand. Very small ones must be sewn by hand because a sewing machine cannot manoeuvre round the edges of such tiny pieces. Fortunately, sewing a miniature bear doesn't take long. It is also possible to sew parts of a bear by machine and other parts, such as the head gusset and foot pads, by hand. This way you can ensure that the stitching is even and a better shape is achieved on these important features.

PATTERNS AND PENS

To use any of the patterns that appear on pages 66–86 you will either have to make a photocopy or trace them directly from the pages of the book using tracing paper and a soft pencil. You will also need some lightweight craft card for turning your copied pattern into workable templates.

To mark out the pattern on the back of the fabric you will need a fine felt-tip permanent marker pen (avoid pencils because they smudge and will make your hands and the fur pile dirty).

SCISSORS

There are usually a few pairs of scissors in every house-hold, but for teddy bear making you will need three different pairs for separate stages of the procedure. First, you will need a pair of general-purpose craft scissors for cutting out your paper and card patterns. For cutting out the pattern pieces from the fabric you will need a pair of dressmaking scissors. A medium-sized pair is better than a large one because of the small sizes and tight curves on some of the pieces.

Finally, a good sharp pair of embroidery scissors is invaluable for trimming threads and the fur on the face when you come to embroider the nose. They are also easier to use when cutting out the pieces for miniature bears. Make sure that all of your scissors are sharp and do not use the wrong pair for a particular task in case it blunts them.

GLUE

Two types of glue are generally used in teddy bear making: an all-purpose craft adhesive suitable for gluing fabric, and white PVA glue. Use the former to attach the felt templates before embroidering the nose and the latter to attach the paper pattern to the craft card.

This can also be diluted with an equal quantity of water to make a cheap fixative for the edges of fabric that have a tendency to fray.

NEEDLES

You will need various different needles to sew your bear by hand. You will find it easier to use a longer needle on the thick fur fabrics. Use one about 65mm (2½in) in length and size 5–7 to oversew the pieces together, stitch them in place and close the seams after stuffing. A large-gauge needle up to around size 14 is needed to embroider the nose, depending on the size of the bear and the embroidery thread chosen. Use a very long and slender needle to attach the glass eyes to the bear's head that will pass through the head easily. These are usually sold as doll-makers needles and are approximately 130mm (5in) in length.

If you are sewing the bear on a sewing machine you will need to use a size 14–16 machine needle. If the fabric you are using has a knitted or jersey backing then it is best to use a ball-point needle. Keep all of your needles in a good sharp condition.

PINS

All of the pieces must be pinned to hold them securely together for stitching. As the fur fabric is so thick, the pins need to be extra long to ensure they stay in position. It is a good idea to buy pins with brightly-coloured plastic or glass heads that are usually sold on a paper or plastic wheel. These are nice and easy to see on the fabric and should also help to prevent any sharp pins being left inside the finished bear. You can see at a glance if any pins are missing from the wheel and may still be in the fabric.

THIMBLE

This is a personal choice as some people find it impossible to sew with a thimble. However, a leather thimble is an excellent way of cushioning your finger when sewing through tough and unyielding areas such as when embroidering the nose. It can also be slipped onto the little finger to stop the strong thread from cutting into your skin when you are sewing up seams that need to be pulled firmly.

PLIERS AND COTTER KEYS

In traditional wooden joints one item is attached to another with a split pin or cotter pin. Once it is in place, this split pin needs to be turned down to secure the joint and this can be done with either good-quality pliers or a cotter key. The pliers should be the long-nosed type and around 15cm (6in) in length. Choose pliers made by a reputable manufacturer that will be strong enough and are less likely to twist in use.

Cotter keys are available from specialist teddy-bear-making suppliers (see page 127). They are exceptionally easy to use and produce very neat joints. They resemble a chunky-handled screwdriver but the end has a precise slot cut into it to take the split pin and has been hardened so that it will not break when in use. Joints turned with cotter keys may be slightly looser than those turned with pliers, so you may need to keep a pair of long-nosed pliers handy to give the joints a final tweak afterwards.

AWL

This tool is invaluable for making holes in the fabric for joints and eyes without causing it to fray, and in cardboard templates to mark key positions. This also looks like a small screwdriver but has a sharp point, which is used to part the weave of the fabric without cutting any of the threads. Other items found around the home such as a knitting needle could also be used.

STUFFING STICKS

Some specialist teddy-bear-making suppliers stock special sticks for stuffing your bear. These have the advantage of an easy-to-grip handle, however more common household items can be used, too. Wooden spoon handles are very handy for packing stuffing into large areas and chopsticks are well suited to small and narrow sections. A wooden manicure stick is very helpful in miniature bear-making – not only for stuffing the bear but also for turning the small completed pieces the right way out.

SAFETY TOOL

The star washers that have to be fixed onto the backs of plastic safety joints and eyes can be difficult to attach with your hands alone. A small metal safety tool which has two different sized holes drilled into it can make the task much easier because it gives you a greater area to push against. The two holes are designed to fit the smaller shanks of the safety eyes as well as the larger ones of the safety joints.

Or you can try this alternative method of securing star washers. Place a cotton reel on top of the washer and tap it with a small hammer.

TEASEL BRUSH

This is an invaluable tool and an absolute must for any bear-maker's toolbox. The most basic teasel brush is a small block of wood onto which short wire bristles are glued or stapled. It is used to free the pile that always becomes trapped in the seams during sewing. Larger teasel brushes with a handle are available from pet shops where they are sold for dog-grooming. These are more comfortable to use than the basic teasel brushes.

A STEP-BY-STEP GUIDE

This step-by-step guide shows you how to make a traditional teddy bear from start to finish using the patterns on pages 66–86. Traditional bears are all made in the same way with a few small exceptions. For example, the bodies are made from either two or four pieces of fabric, and the limbs from either a single folded piece or two separate ones that are stitched together. Details of how to deal with these differences in design are included in the steps.

The letters A–H refer to points marked on the patterns. A 6mm (¼in) seam allowance is included in the patterns and should be used throughout. It is best to pin and oversew (see page 23) the seams together before sewing them, instead of tacking (basting). When using a sewing machine, stitch the seams twice to make them really strong (see also Stitching Seams on page 24) and use a fixative to neaten them. Ladder stitch (see page 16) is the only other stitch required.

MAKING THE TEMPLATES

First you will need to make a copy of all the pattern pieces for your chosen bear from the pattern section on pages 66–86. This can be done either by tracing the pieces or by photocopying them. Paste the paper pattern onto some lightweight craft card (cereal boxes are a good substitute) and cut them out. It is also a good idea to cut all of the reverse pieces from card so that mistakes are not made when marking the back of

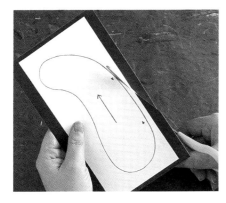

your fabric. Make sure that you include all of the relevant pattern information such as joint and limb positions on your card templates. If you intend to make several versions of the same teddy bear, cut all of the pattern pieces from semi-transparent plastic sheets which you can buy from specialist teddy-bear-making suppliers (see page 127).

MARKING THE FABRIC

Before you start marking the back of your fabric you need to establish which way the pile lies. Stroke the fabric in different directions: it will feel the smoothest when you are following the pile. Mark this direction with an arrow on the back of the fabric so that you can identify it again when laying out the templates. On some fabrics, especially those with a distressed

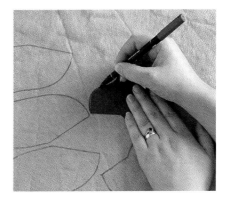

finish, the pile direction will be random. With these it is best to follow the general pile direction. Take extra care when marking out the head and head gusset pieces as these should be laid so that the arrow on the pattern follows the pile on that area of the fabric.

Lay all the pattern pieces onto the back of the fabric so that the arrows on the templates follow the pile direction. Draw around each piece using a fine marker pen and include the relevant information such as joint positions. At the same time mark out the paws and pads onto felt or other pad fabric.

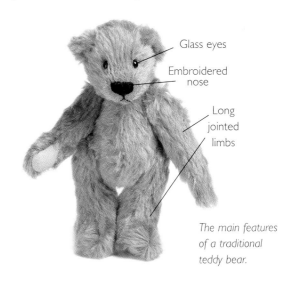

Glass eyes

Embroidered nose

Long jointed limbs

The main features of a traditional teddy bear.

CUTTING OUT

Lay the fabric out fur side down on a clean flat surface ready for cutting. With all pile fabrics it is essential that only the backing fabric and none of the pile is cut, so great care must be taken over cutting. Using sharp dressmaking scissors, slide the points of the scissors between the pile so that they are level with

the backing fabric. Make small snipping cuts around the outline of the pieces taking care not to cut through the pile at any stage. When all of the pieces have been cut out take a little time to pair the relevant pieces together and make sure you have cut the correct number of limbs or other body pieces. Keep a small piece of the fabric to check your sewing machine tension before you start making up your teddy bear.

MAKING THE HEAD

The head is probably the most complex part of a teddy bear because it requires three pieces to create its shape. However, it is not difficult to make. Pin the two head pieces right sides together and oversew in place from points A to B on the pattern. Remove the pins and stitch. Now pin the head gusset in place with right sides together. First pin the gusset to the eye area, marked C on the pattern, on each side. Insert the next

pin at the tip of the nose A, then add more pins in between to hold this nose area securely in place. Line up the bottom edges at point D and continue pinning until the entire gusset is held in position. Oversew the seams to secure them, remove the pins and stitch in place. The head can now be turned right side out.

MAKING THE ARMS

Lay a felt paw piece onto one of the inner arm pieces so that points E and F match and the straight edges are level. Oversew the paw pad in position, remove the pins and stitch in place. Now complete the arm: on a design with a two-piece arm, lay the inner arm on top of the corresponding outer arm right with sides together

and pin in position. Use the pins to tuck in as much of the fur as possible to keep the seams tidy. On a folded arm design, simply fold the arm in half with right sides together and pin in position. Oversew in place, remove the pins and stitch together, remembering to leave the opening for turning marked on the pattern. This will be at the back of the arm on a two-piece arm and at the front on a folded design. Turn right side out and repeat for the other arm.

MAKING THE LEGS

On a design such as Anastasia (page 58) that has a two-piece leg, pin two leg pieces right sides together. Oversew the leg, remove the pins and stitch this seam, remembering to leave the bottom foot edge and the opening marked on the pattern for turning unstitched. On a design that has a single folded leg piece, fold the leg in half right sides together and continue as above, leaving the gap for turning at the front of the leg as marked on the pattern.

Now take one of the foot pads and fold in half lengthways, pressing along the fold to leave a crease. Open it out again and pin it to the bottom edge of

the leg matching the heel and toe seams to the crease in the foot pad. Continue pinning until it is secured and oversew in position. Remove the pins and stitch the foot pad in place. You may find it easier to do this by hand to achieve an even shape. Turn the leg right side out and repeat for the other leg.

MAKING THE BODY

To make the body on a four-piece design such as Mei Ying (page 52), pin a front body piece to a back body piece right sides together along the side seam from points G to H. Oversew in position, remove the pins and stitch in place. Repeat this with the other front and back body pieces. These two new pieces can then be pinned together to complete the body. First match

the seams at the top and bottom of the body then continue pinning until the seams are firmly held in position. Oversew in place, remove the pins and stitch.

On a two-piece design such as Georgie (page 30), first stitch the darts at the top and bottom of the body. Fold each body piece in half lengthways with right sides together and stitch along the straight dart line at the top and bottom of the body. Pin the completed pieces together matching the darts and oversew in position. Remove the pins, stitch securely in place and turn the body right side out.

MAKING THE EARS

The ears are the only parts of the bear that now still need to be stitched. These can be a little awkward to sew on a small bear so it may be best to stitch them by hand. Pin two of the ear pieces right sides together around the curved edge, tucking in as much of the fur as you can. Oversew the edges together to hold them firmly in place. Remove the pins and stitch the ear pieces

together around the curved edge leaving the straight edge open. Turn the ear right side out. Tuck under the raw edges at the bottom of the ear to neaten them and oversew together. Repeat for the remaining ear. On larger bears you can partially-stitch the bottom straight edges together, leaving a gap in the centre for turning. This makes it easier to finish the raw edges at the bottom of the ear, but it is important to turn the ears properly by pushing out the fabric at the corners.

STUFFING AND JOINTING THE HEAD

Where used, plastic safety eyes must be fixed in position before the head can be stuffed. Make a small hole with the awl at the point where you want each eye to go and insert the shank. From the inside of the head attach the safety washer to secure each eye in place.

When stuffing any part of your bear, always fill the area furthest away from the opening first. On the head this is the nose. Fill the nose area as firmly as possible so that the fabric will not pucker and pull out of shape when the nose is embroidered. Insert the head joint when the head is completely filled. Lay the half of the joint with the split pin on top of the filler making sure that none of the filler comes over the side. Using strong thread, run a gathering stitch around the neck edge and pull up the opening so that it gathers around the split pin. Finish off securely.

STUFFING AND JOINTING THE LIMBS

The joints should be inserted before the limbs are stuffed. Joint positions are marked on the pattern and these should be transferred when the pattern is marked on the back of the fabric. Make a small hole in the fabric with the awl at each joint position and

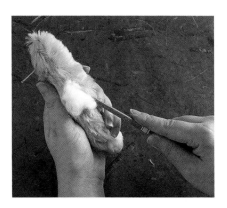

insert the half joint with the split pin. Joint positions will have been marked on both sides of the leg so make sure that you create a pair of legs by inserting the joints in the opposite side of each leg.

The limbs can now be stuffed by filling the area furthest from the opening first. How hard you stuff them is up to you, but traditional bears were usually very firmly stuffed. Close the opening with ladder stitch once the limb is filled.

CLOSING A SEAM WITH LADDER STITCH

All of the openings on the bear should be closed neatly and securely using ladder stitch. Thread a needle with strong thread and knot the end. Starting at the top of the opening, insert the needle from the inside edge and pull the thread through so that the knot is on the inside. Make the first stitch horizontally

across to the opposite side of the opening. Take a small stitch along, before taking another one horizontally across to the other side of the opening. Continue working in this way down the entire length of the opening, pulling the stitches tight as you go to close the seam. The stitches should be parallel to prevent the fabric from puckering and looking unsightly. Finish off by making a knot at the base of the seam then lose the thread end by inserting the needle directly next to the knot and emerging a short distance away. Pull the thread tightly and snip off as close to the fabric as possible. The thread end will then disappear into the limb.

EMBROIDERING THE NOSE

Cut out the nose template from felt that matches the nose thread (see page 9) you will be using. Trim away the fur in the nose area that will be directly under the template. Using all-purpose craft glue (see page 11),

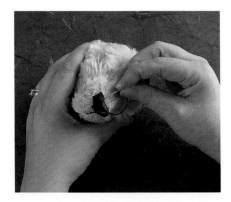

stick the template in position and leave to dry. Thread a needle with nose thread and take a few stitches behind the template (A, B and C in the diagram right) to secure the end, inserting the needle into the same hole it emerged from. Follow the diagram, keeping the stitches as close together as possible and completely

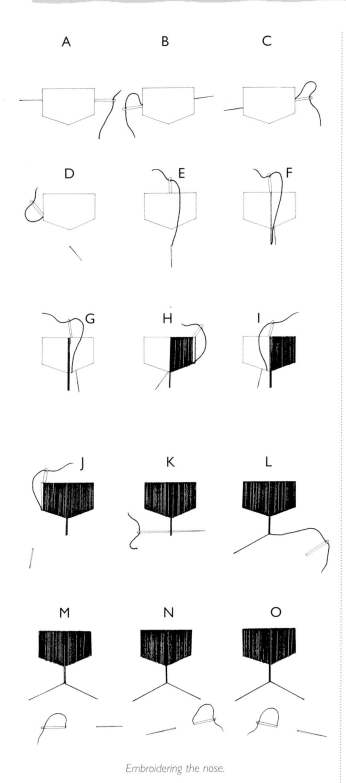

A B C

D E F

G H I

J K L

M N O

Embroidering the nose.

covering the template. At J bring the needle out at one end of the mouth, pass the needle under the long centre stitch and insert it again directly opposite to complete the mouth, checking that it is level. Secure the thread to finish off in the same way as when starting and snip close to the fabric.

ATTACHING EARS

The positioning of the ears can make a great difference to the character of your bear. Placing them high on a bear's head can make it look alert; putting them low down can create a more cheeky character. Pin the first ear to the head so that the top edge of the ear is level with the head gusset seam and continue pinning the

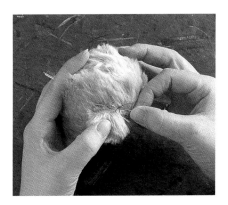

ear to the head in a curved position. Repeat with the other ear on the opposite side of the head making sure that they are level. Now take a good look at the bear and decide if the ears are in the right position. If you are not happy it is easy to change them at this stage. Move them around until you are happy with the positioning. Ladder stitch them securely in place using strong thread.

ATTACHING GLASS EYES

Cut a length of strong thread that will be long enough when doubled to pass through the bear's head and leave plenty spare for tying off. Pass the looped end of the thread through the loop of the glass eye, then push the two thread ends back through the thread loop and pull tight so that the thread is securely fixed to the eye. Thread the two ends onto the long dollmakers needle. Close up the loop of the eye with pliers so that it fits into the head easily. Make a small

hole with the awl where you want the eye to go and insert the needle in it, pushing it through the head to emerge at the back in the centre, as close as possible to the base. Leave the threads hanging while you insert the other eye in the same way. Bring the needle out 1cm (½in) away from the first set of threads. Make sure that the eyes are level and equally spaced before pulling the thread ends as tightly as you can and knotting them together to secure the eyes in position.

TURNING A WOODEN JOINT PIN

Before you go on to assemble your teddy bear you need to know how to fix the joints in position. On a traditional wooden joint the split pin must be turned down so that it rests on the metal washer, to stop the pin from wearing through the wooden disc when the limb is moved. Grip the top of the longer split pin tightly with long-nosed pliers or a cotter key as

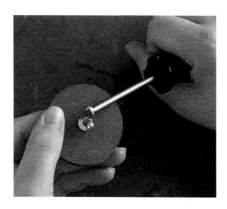

shown, and turn it outwards and down so that the tip is turned back on itself and is touching a little way down. Grip the split pin again, this time at the top of the coil and turn it down further. Continue in this way until the coiled split pin rests on the metal washer. Repeat this procedure on the other split pin so that it rests on the metal washer, too. Practise turning the split pins on spare joints until you are confident you can secure the pins firmly and neatly.

ATTACHING THE HEAD

The head is the first item to be attached to the body. It should already have its joint fitted. On the inside of the body, find the head-joint position that was marked on the pattern and make a small hole here with the awl. Make sure that you do not make this hole through any seams as this will weaken the stitching and may cause the seam to break open. If your

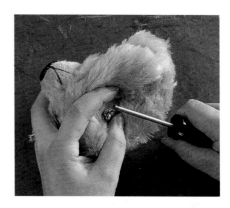

stitching passes through this mark, make the hole slightly to one side, but as close to the original mark as possible. Pass the split pin through this hole from the outside of the body. Thread a wooden disc onto the split pin followed by a metal washer from the inside of the body. The split pin can now be turned down as tightly as possible so that it rests on the metal washer.

ATTACHING THE LIMBS

The arms and legs are attached in a similar way to the head. Find the marks for the arm joint positions on the inside of the body and make a small hole with the awl. Pass the split pin through this hole from the outside of the body and thread the wooden disc and then the metal washer onto it from the inside of the body. Turn the split pin down securely and repeat with the other arm. Attach the legs in exactly the

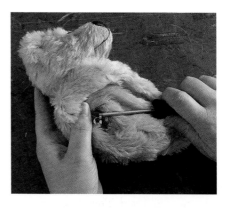

same way ensuring that the split pins are turned down so that they rest on the metal washer. When all of the limbs and the head are attached, take time to move each one in turn to see if the joints are tight enough. It is much easier to adjust any of the joints now rather than when the bear is finished. Moving the joints will also flatten the fur between them, which may make the joint feel a little looser. If this happens simply tighten the joints a little more with pliers.

STUFFING THE BODY
AND ADDING A GROWLER

Once the joints have been checked the bear's body can be filled. Begin filling the bear at the neck area ensuring that the area between the neck and arm joints is firmly stuffed. Continue stuffing the body with your chosen filling until you are happy with the way your bear looks.

If you intend to add pellets, glass beads or steel shot to add extra weight or give your bear a saggy look (see page 10), you should still use a little

polyester or other soft filling to stuff the neck area. This will ensure that the bear can hold his head up. Fill the body with as much pellet filling as required to give the bear the correct appearance you want. Using fewer pellets will make the bear 'sag' as though he is very old and his filling has collapsed.

To add a voice to your bear, use polyester stuffing to fill the bear at the neck, bottom and front of the tummy. Lay the growler horizontally in the tummy with the holes facing you. Pack filling firmly around the growler so that it will not move and cannot be felt from the outside. Close the back seam with ladder stitch (see page 16).

EMBROIDERING CLAWS

You can give extra detail to your bear by embroidering claws on its paws and feet. These are easy to add and usually appear as four equally spaced claws. Thread the needle used to embroider the nose with a length of nose thread. Secure the end of the thread in the same way as for embroidering the nose (see page 17) by passing the needle from one side of the top of the paw to the other then inserting it back into the hole it has just emerged from. Continue in this way until the thread is secure. Bring the needle out on the felt pad at the start of the first claw. Make one long stitch

across the pad into the fur on the end of the foot. Bring the needle out at the start of the second claw and make another long stitch across the foot. Continue in this way until you have embroidered the desired number of claws. Secure the thread to finish off in the same way as when starting.

GROOMING THE
FINISHED BEAR

Before your teddy bear is complete, he will need to be spruced up with a teasel brush and some final trimming of the fur. Brush along each seam against the direction of the pile so that any trapped fur will be lifted out of it. Be very careful when brushing around the eyes, because the wire bristles can easily scratch

the shiny surface of glass eyes. Also take care around the embroidered nose and claws, as well as the pads, especially if they are made from felt.

Some of the fur may need to be trimmed especially if you have used a long-pile fur. The muzzle area is usually trimmed so that the eyes are not obscured by excessive fur. Use a pair of small pointed embroidery scissors to gradually trim away the pile following the direction of the fur. You may also wish to trim away some of the pile to reveal details such as the claws on the feet and paws.

DRESSING THE BEARS

S o now it's time to dress your teddy bear. It really doesn't matter if you've never made a garment before. In this chapter you will find all the information you need to create the outfits in this book. There are details of the materials and essential equipment you need, followed by a comprehensive guide to the basic dressmaking techniques used. Each step is illustrated by a photograph, and there are diagrams to explain the stitches.

MATERIALS

From cotton to crepe de chine and velvet to viscose, there are so many different dressmaking fabrics to choose from that it would take a whole book to describe them all. While any of these fabrics can be used for a full-sized garment, the thickness of the cloth or the size of the pattern makes many of them unsuitable for teddy-bear clothes.

When buying fabrics always keep in mind the scale of the garment you are making. As the bears are quite small it is advisable to choose a fabric printed with a small design so that the pattern can be seen to its full advantage. Most of the outfits that appear in this book were made from pure cotton or polyester-cotton printed fabric. These fabrics are available in numerous designs and colours and range in price from very cheap to fairly expensive. They are easy to sew and ideal for newcomers to dressmaking.

Cotton fabrics are also perfect for garments that need to be gathered, which is the easiest and most commonly used method of fitting for these designs.

Full details of the fabrics we used for the outfits are included with each design, leaving you to decide on the colour and pattern and let your imagination run wild.

OTHER TYPES OF FABRIC USED

Woven and woollen fabrics are suitable for teddy-bear outfits provided the weave is not too open and lightweight types such as flannel are chosen. These fabrics can be quite expensive, but they will play an important part in making an outfit look right.

Satin fabrics and velvets are used to great effect on several garments. Satin fabrics are quite easy to sew but velvets can cause problems for a novice. Panné velvet is the easiest velvet of all to sew. This drapes very well and has a knitted backing. Although it may seem rather thin, it is perfectly adequate when a lining has been inserted.

Several outfits such as Georgie's duffel coat (page 34) and Grandpa's waistcoat

When you are dressing teddy bears, choose fabrics printed with a small pattern that will be clearly visible on clothes made to this scale.

(page 46) are lined. Lining fabric is available in many different colours and qualities, but it is not necessary to spend a fortune on this fabric as teddy-bear clothes will not be subjected to heavy wear. Lining fabrics should be handled as little as possible because they fray and the seams should be neatened or treated with a fixative to prevent the cut edges from fraying.

Use fusible interfacing when the fabric needs stiffening, for example to make Grandpa's slippers (page 46). Use very firm interfacing for these. If you think the fabric you have chosen for another garment would benefit from extra support, buy interfacing that is lighter and softer than the fabric. Fusible interfacing is pressed onto the wrong side of the fabric using a damp cloth and a dry iron. Try out the interfacing on a scrap of fabric first to make sure that the material does not stiffen too much and spoil the overall effect.

A few of the garments have a lace trimming added to the sleeves or hems. Of the many types of lace available for this purpose we used a narrow lace with a straight top edge. If you want to be adventurous you could use a lace fabric to make a garment such as Anastasia's ball gown (page 58) and turn it into a wedding dress. When cutting out pattern pieces from lace you do not have to worry about the grain direction (see page 23). Instead, look at the pattern of the lace and position the pieces accordingly.

THREADS

For basic dressmaking you only need three different types of thread.

TACKING (BASTING) THREAD

The fabric pieces must be tacked (basted) in position to hold them together ready for sewing. A tacking or basting thread is used for this. This soft, unfinished thread is slightly fluffy and grips the layers of fabric.

Once the fabric has been sewn, the tacking (basting) thread can be easily removed without damaging the material. As this is a soft thread, it has no strength and should not be used for permanent stitching.

SEWING THREADS

There are several types of sewing thread suitable for permanent stitching to choose from. Pick one that matches your fabric. If you are using pure cotton your sewing thread should contain cotton fibres, so try either a mercerised cotton thread or a cotton-covered polyester thread. If you are using a synthetic fabric, choose a thread made from synthetic fibres, for example Drima – a spun polyester thread. This is a stronger thread than cotton and can be used on any type of fabric whatever its fibre content. It is also possible to buy silk thread if you are splashing out on your teddy bear's outfit by using a silk fabric.

BUTTONHOLE THREAD

For really neat and professional buttonholes, consider using a buttonhole thread. This thread is thicker than ordinary sewing thread and makes it much easier to sew buttonholes by hand. It can also be used in the sewing machine with a bobbin below filled with normal sewing thread.

FASTENINGS

Whatever style of garment you are making you'll find a button to match: an enormous amount of different sizes, colours and styles are available. Even if you cannot find exactly what you need it is possible to buy button blanks, ready to be covered with the fabric of your choice.

Velcro is the trade name for the hook-and-loop fastener. This is made up of two halves: one has hooks woven onto the nylon tape and the other side has loops. When the two sides are pressed together, the fastening is incredibly strong. It can be used in place of any other recommended closure and is ideal for replacing buttons and buttonholes. It comes in different widths but can be trimmed to size without fraying. Self-adhesive Velcro should not be used on fabrics.

ESSENTIAL EQUIPMENT

TAPE MEASURE

This may sound like a basic piece of equipment but it is essential for placing pattern pieces correctly on the fabric. Make sure that your tape measure is easy to read and in good condition. Consider buying a new one if it is frayed and stretched.

MARKING PENCIL

On fine fabrics use a chalk marking pencil instead of a marker pen like the one we used to transfer the pattern onto the back of the mohair fabric (see page 13). The chalk can be removed later either by brushing it away or by washing the finished garment. The pencil blunts easily and should be sharpened regularly to ensure that a clear, well-defined line is produced. Fabric pens are also available and can usually be removed with water. Try out your pencil or other marker on a scrap of fabric first.

SCISSORS

As in bear-making (see page 11), a pair of good quality, sharp dressmaking scissors is recommended for making teddy-bear clothes. These make cutting out the fabric much easier and more accurate. If you need to buy a new pair, check they are comfortable and the finger holes do not cause any discomfort. Small embroidery scissors are useful for snipping threads and for unpicking seams if you make a mistake. Pinking shears are handy for finishing the edges of seams on fabrics that do not fray readily. These scissors make zigzag cuts along the edge of the fabric: space the zigzags evenly so that they do not overlap.

PINS

Use ordinary steel pins for dressmaking instead of the long pins with coloured heads needed for bear-making. Good quality steel dressmaking pins are a wise investment as they are sharp and will not snag or damage the fabric. They are available in different thicknesses: use finer pins for delicate fabrics such as silk. Throw away any pins that have started to rust.

NEEDLES

A needle is a basic piece of dressmaking equipment. The best ones to use for hand sewing are known as 'betweens'. These are shorter than other needles, which makes it easier for you to produce small, even stitches. When you need to sew together several bulky layers of fabric, however, a between won't be long enough. Instead, use one of the longer 'sharps'.

When choosing the size of your needle, pick one that matches both the fabric and the thread you are using. It should make a hole in the fabric just large enough for the thread to follow. If this hole is too big, the fabric will not grip the thread and the stitch will be too loose. If this hole is too small, the thread will not pass through the fabric easily and may damage it. Generally, the closer the weave of the fabric, the smaller the needle required.

A STEP-BY-STEP GUIDE

There are many different dressmaking techniques to choose from, however all of the outfits in this book are made using a few simple procedures and stitches. Even if you have never made a garment before you should be able to tackle any of the projects with confidence using this step-by-step guide. All of the pattern pieces have a 6mm (¼in) seam allowance included. All the stitches used are shown below.

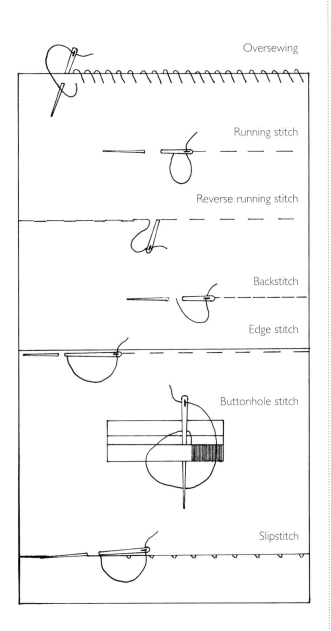

Oversewing

Running stitch

Reverse running stitch

Backstitch

Edge stitch

Buttonhole stitch

Slipstitch

Shown above are all the stitches you will need to handsew the bears and their outfits.

FINDING THE GRAIN AND MARKING THE FABRIC

For best results, line up each pattern piece with the straight grain of the fabric. This runs parallel to the selvage. The grain line is marked on the pattern with an arrow. Fold the fabric in half with right sides and the selvage edges together. Lay the pattern pieces on

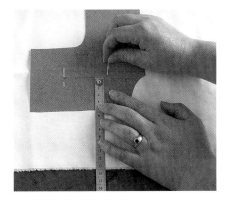

top, putting any marked 'cut on fold' along the fold as directed. Line up the other pieces to follow the grain by measuring from one end of the grain-line arrow to the selvage. Measure from the other end of the grain line to the selvage and adjust the pattern until both measurements are the same. Pin the pattern in place on a double layer of fabric or draw around it using a marking pencil if only one piece is required. Transfer all of the markings on the pattern to the fabric at this stage. When everything is complete cut out the pieces.

PINNING

Before fabric pieces can be sewn together they need to be held in place with pins. Place the fabric pieces together as required and pin together along the seams

that are to be stitched. Space the pins about 5–10cm (2–4in) apart and insert them so that the points are nearest the edge of the fabric in the seam allowance. This makes it easier to remove them once the pieces have been tacked (basted) in position. Make sure, too, that the pins are inserted at right angles to the edge of the fabric. Then the sewing machine needle will easily pass over them if you intend to sew the seams without tacking (basting) them first. Newcomers to dressmaking are advised to include this step before sewing.

TACKING OR BASTING

Tack (baste) the pinned fabric pieces in position to hold them securely for stitching. Thread a needle with a length of tacking (basting) thread (see page 21) and knot the end. Position your tacking (basting) just inside the seam line so that the stitches will be easy to remove later. Use a large running stitch (see page 23)

making the stitches about 6mm (¼in) long and about 6mm (¼in) apart. When you reach the end of the seam make a couple of stitches on top of each other to secure the thread. Tacking (basting) can also be worked on a sewing machine. Set the machine to its longest stitch length and sew just inside the seam line. This method is quicker and is especially useful when attaching three or more layers in stages, for example in making the hood on Anastasia's cloak (page 58).

STITCHING SEAMS

Once the fabric pieces are tacked (basted) together the seam can be stitched. If you are using a sewing machine, first test the tension and stitch length on a scrap of fabric. Set your machine on a medium length stitch to sew mohair and on a smaller stitch to sew cotton dressmaking fabrics.

When your machine is set correctly, put the needle into the fabric on the seam line about 12mm (½in)

away from the edge of the fabric. Lower the presser foot which should be level with the raw edges of the fabric and stitch backwards to the edge to secure the ends of the thread. Stitch forwards keeping to the seam line until you reach the other end of the seam. Stitch backwards again for about 12mm (½in) to finish off and trim the thread ends.

If you are sewing by hand, thread your needle with sewing thread and start the seam with a few backstitches to secure. This stitch is worked in a 'one step backwards, two steps forward' motion (see diagram on page 23). Continue sewing the seam in backstitch or reverse running stitch, finishing off securely at the other end. Press the completed seam open.

TRIMMING AND CLIPPING SEAMS

As the dressmaking designs in this book only use a small seam allowance (6mm/¼in), you shouldn't have to trim any straight flat seams before neatening them. Sometimes, however, you will have to trim a seam to reduce its bulk, for example if the seam will be pressed to one side because it joins a skirt to a bodice, or if the seam is enclosed in a collar. Where sharp corners have been created the seam allowance needs to be trimmed at the points so that a ridge won't

form after turning. If the fabric is particularly thick or there are more than two layers of fabric, the seam allowance should be graded to help the seam lie flat and prevent ridges from forming. Trim each layer of the seam to a different width, making the top layer the narrowest and the bottom layer the widest. If the seam is curved it will need to be clipped to help it lie flat. Use scissors to make snips in the seam allowance up to the stitching line.

NEATENING SEAMS

When the seam is complete the raw edges must be neatened to stop them from fraying. This can be achieved by oversewing the raw edges by machine or by hand. Modern sewing machines have various stitches that can be used to neaten seams: the most popular one is a basic zigzag. Test the stitch length

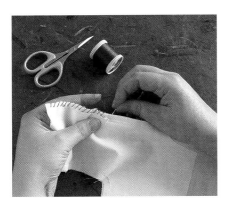

and width on your machine on a scrap of the fabric before zigzagging close to the seam. If your machine can only do a straight stitch, fold the seam to the outside so that the raw edge is level with the seam stitching, then edge stitch close to the fold. If you prefer to sew by hand, the edges can be neatened by oversewing (page 23). Insert the needle at right angles to the edge of the fabric and take diagonal stitches over the raw edge keeping the stitches the same distance apart and of a consistent depth.

FACINGS

Facings are often used as a way of neatening the neck edge and the front or back opening edges of a garment. The two front or back facings are stitched right sides together to the neck facing at the shoulder seams. The outer edge is neatened and the completed facing is stitched to the garment with right sides together matching the shoulder seams. When the facing is stitched in place the corners are trimmed and

the curved edge clipped to stop the seam from being strained. The facing can now be turned to the inside, making sure that the corners are pushed through, and pressed. To hold the facing in position on the inside of the garment, tack (baste) the edges to the seam allowance of the garment's shoulder seam. This is all that is needed to finish the facing but if you would like to add extra detail, edge stitch around the neck edge and along the front or back opening.

GATHERING

Gathering stitches are used when a large piece of fabric is joined to a much smaller piece and a large amount of fullness has to be controlled. This usually occurs when joining a skirt to a bodice or with inset sleeves. To gather using hand stitching, make two rows of large running stitches (page 23) where directed. Make the first row of stitches on the seam line and

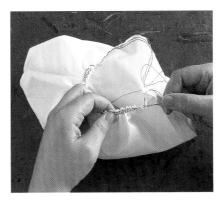

the second row about 3mm (⅛in) away in the seam allowance. Do not secure either ends of the threads but leave a fairly long tail for pulling up the gathers. Pull the thread ends and push the fabric along the thread so that it forms gathers until it is the right size to fit the garment. Pin the gathered piece to the garment and adjust the gathers so that they are evenly spaced, then tack (baste) and stitch in place.

HEMMING

When the garment is finished the final task is to hem the bottom raw edge. As a rule, a 12mm (½in) hem has been included in the patterns but this is only a guide. Put the garment onto your bear to determine the required finished length. Mark the length with pins and remove the garment carefully. Press the hem to the wrong side along this line so that there is an obvious

crease. Open out the hem and turn under again so that the raw edge is level with the crease and press in place. Turn the hem back up along the original crease so that the raw edge is enclosed and slipstitch or edge stitch (page 23) in place. If the garment has a facing attached, turn the bottom edge of the facing to the outside and stitch in place along the hemline. Trim the seam and press the facing back to the inside. The hem can now be completed as before.

SLIPSTITCH

This is an invaluable stitch to learn as it can be used anywhere you do not want your stitching to show, for example on hems or when attaching a lining. Thread your needle with sewing thread and secure the end using backstitch in an area that will not show on the front of the garment. Insert the needle into the folded

edge of the hem and slide it along to emerge about 12mm (½in) away, pulling the thread through. Pick up a single thread of the fabric underneath directly above where the needle has emerged. Only pick up one thread because this will be visible on the front of the garment. Insert the needle back into the fold of the hem next to where the needle first emerged and pull the thread through so that a small v-shaped stitch is formed. Bring the needle out another 12mm (½in) away and continue working in this way until the hem is securely stitched in place.

INSERTING SLEEVES

On many of the bears' outfits, the sleeves and body of the garment are cut as one piece, however some, for example Anastasia's ballgown on page 58, have set-in sleeves. The body of the garment should be stitched together at the shoulder and side seams before the sleeves are inserted. The sleeve is then gathered at the top and bottom edges, the underarm seam stitched and the sleeve bands attached. With right sides together,

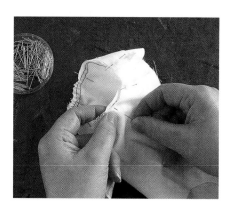

pin the sleeve to the armhole of the garment matching the underarm seams and the top of the sleeve with the shoulder seam. Gather the sleeve evenly so that it fits into the armhole and tack (baste) in place. Stitch the sleeve in place and neaten the seam by oversewing or zigzag stitching (see page 25) the layers together. Repeat with the other sleeve and turn the garment right side out. None of the gathering stitches should now be visible but they can be removed if necessary. Press the seam towards the sleeve to finish.

WAISTBANDS

A waistband is needed where a degree of fullness has to be incorporated, such as on a skirt. To make the waistband, fold the fabric in half lengthways with right sides together and press to make a crease. Press under the seam allowance to the wrong side on one of the long edges. Sew a seam down both short edges, trim the corners and turn right side out. Pin the waistband in place around the top of the skirt, with wrong sides together, matching the raw edges and the opening edge of the skirt with the short edge of the waistband. At the

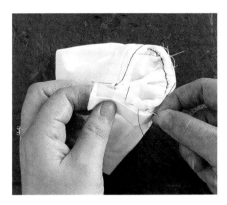

other end, a small part of the waistband will now extend past the opening. Sew the waistband in place and press the seam towards the waistband. The waistband can now be turned so that the long edge you pressed earlier lies directly over the seam. Slipstitch in place (see page 26). Make a buttonhole (see page 28) in the waistband extension and sew on a button to meet it.

MAKING AND ATTACHING BIAS BINDING

Bias binding is available in many colours and widths but you may prefer to make your own for a special garment. Fold down the top corner of a rectangular piece of fabric diagonally so that it meets the bottom edge. This is known as the true bias of the fabric. Using this as a guide, mark out and cut a series of parallel strips of the desired width; each end will be a diagonal. If the binding is not long enough two strips can be joined with a seam. Stitch the strips together with right sides facing so that they are at right angles:

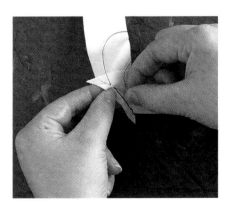

the points should extend beyond the strips. Press the seam open and trim off the triangular ends. Fold the binding wrong side together and press down the crease, stretching it gently to remove any slack. Attach the binding to the edge of the garment in the same way as a waistband.

MAKING AND ATTACHING COLLARS

A collar can enhance a plain garment by providing extra detail. A simple one-piece folded collar is most suited to the petite outfits designed for teddy bears in this book. Fold the collar piece in half lengthways with right sides together and matching the raw edges; press in position. Press under the seam allowance to the wrong side on one of the long edges. Stitch a seam down the two short edges of the collar; trim the

corners, turn and press. With right sides together, pin the collar in position along the neck of the garment matching the edge of the collar with the finished edge of the front opening of the garment. Stitch in place and press the seam up towards the collar. Turn the collar up and press to the inside so that the long edge pressed earlier lies directly over the seam; slipstitch in place (see opposite).

LINING

A lining can be attached to almost any garment to make an outfit more special. Cut out the pattern pieces from the lining material (see page 21) and make them up following the same instructions as for the original garment.

On coats and tops, pin the lining right sides together around the outer edges of the garment. Tuck the arms of the lining into the arms of the garment to keep them out of the way of the seams. Stitch the lining in place leaving a gap in the bottom edge for turning.

Trim the corners of the seams and pull the arms of the garment out so that you can slipstitch (page 26) the pressed edges of the lining to the sleeve from the inside. Turn the right way out.

On skirts or trousers, make up the garment and the lining in the same way and turn both right sides out. Tack (baste) the lining to the inside of the garment with wrong sides together before attaching the waistband or turning the waist edge over to finish.

BUTTONHOLES

To work a buttonhole by hand, make small running stitches about 3mm (⅛in) away from either side of the buttonhole marking on the pattern and across both ends. Using sharp pointed scissors, carefully slash inside these stitched lines to make the buttonhole. Now thread your needle with buttonhole thread, secure the end on the wrong side of the fabric with a

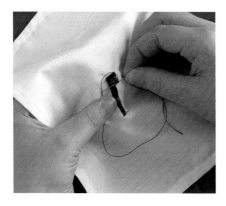

few backstitches, and bring it to the right side. Work buttonhole stitch by inserting the needle through the slash from the right side and bringing it back out again on the outside of the running stitches (see also page 23). Pass the needle through the loop of thread that is formed and pull the stitch to gently tighten the knot that is created at the edge of the buttonhole. Continue working in this way, keeping your stitches

and the knots at the edge of the buttonhole even. To finish the ends, take 3 or 4 long stitches across the width of the buttonhole then work buttonhole stitch over the top of these through all the layers of fabric. If you are using a sewing machine, stitch the buttonhole before slashing through the buttonhole marking.

ATTACHING VELCRO

If you find the thought of sewing buttonholes and attaching buttons too daunting, all of the openings on the outfits can be closed using Velcro instead. Cut the Velcro into one long strip to fit the opening. Sew on the hook section first, to the under side of the opening

keeping your line of stitches as close to the edge as possible. This can be done with a sewing machine or by hand in backstitch, if you do not mind the stitches showing. If you prefer your stitches to be invisible, pin the Velcro and slipstitch it in place or use small over-sewing stitches around the edges. Attach the loop section to the overlapping part of the opening in the same way. You can also cut the Velcro into small squares and stitch them in place making sure they are evenly spaced. If you want your garment to look the same as one that has buttonholes, sew a button over each square of Velcro on the outside.

ATTACHING LACE

Most lace comes with pre-finished edges, so there's no need to worry about it fraying. It also has one straight edge. It is easiest to attach the lace to a garment before it is sewn together. Pin the lace to the edge of the fabric with right sides facing and matching the straight edge of the lace to the raw edge. Stitch in place and press the seam towards the garment. This can now be made up following the instructions. If you want to add a lace trim to a finished garment,

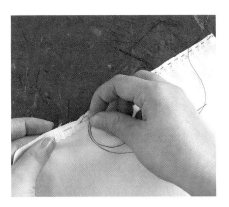

measure the edge of the garment accurately and add a further 12mm (½in) for the seam allowance. Cut the lace to this length, then with right sides facing, fold the lace in half and stitch the two short edges together. Pin the lace onto the garment with the wrong side of the lace facing the right side of the fabric and stitch in place.

PATCH POCKETS

You can attach pockets to almost any garment as an extra detail. Patch pockets are much the easiest type to incorporate into an outfit and can be made in any size or shape you like. Press the seam allowance to the wrong side along each edge of the pocket. Stitch

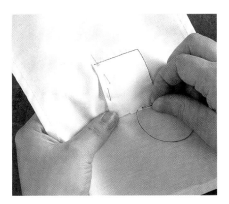

in place along the top edge only using slipstitch (page 26) if you do not want the stitches to be visible on the outside of the pocket. Position the pocket on the garment and pin in place making sure that it is level. Stitch the pocket to the garment either by machine or by hand using backstitch and keeping the stitches as close to the edge as possible.

If you want to add any further pockets to the same garment, make sure they are positioned parallel to the first one. Sew the patch pockets in place before the lining is attached to the garment. This will ensure the stitching is hidden on the inside.

PRESSING AND FINISHING THE GARMENT

When the outfit has been sewn together and has been tried on the bear, it is worth spending a few minutes checking and finishing off properly. First, check each seam, trim off any loose thread ends and remove any tacking (basting) stitches that may have been missed. If the garment has become slightly grubby during sewing or you have used a fabric marker pen that

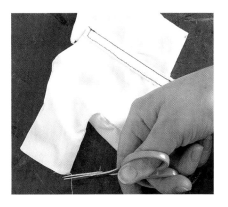

needs to be washed out, gently hand-wash the outfit in warm water and mild detergent. Even if the garment does not need washing the outfit will still need pressing to make it look professional. Press each garment on the wrong side of the fabric, to avoid creating a shine on the right side. If it is necessary to press the right side of the fabric always use a cloth of the same type of fabric between the garment and the iron. When pressing gathers, hold the fabric along the stitching and use the tip of the iron to press between the folds of the fabric. For curved areas use a rolled up thick towel so that unwanted creases do not form.

Turn to page 36 for details of how to make this dress for Georgie.

GEORGIE

Named after my niece Georgie, I'm sure this endearing little bear will soon find a place in your heart, too. It's an ideal mascot for someone who's starting college or facing important exams, and is sure to become a firm friend. Make your Georgie a boy or a girl and dress them in one of the six charming outfits that are all sewn from a few simple pattern pieces. This well-dressed bear's wardrobe includes dungarees, dresses and a duffel coat, so you can easily create your own special look.

It should only take you a couple of evenings to make and dress Georgie in your chosen clothes, so this is an ideal first bear-making project to try. It's also perfect for those times when you want a special gift at short notice.

TO MAKE GEORGIE

- ▶ 50 × 40cm (20 × 16in) 12mm (½in) pile, soft distressed English mohair fabric
- ▶ Five, 25mm (1in) traditional wooden or safety joints
- ▶ One pair 6mm (¼in) black glass (or plastic safety) eyes
- ▶ 20 × 20cm (8 × 8in) felt for the paws
- ▶ 1m (40in) black perle cotton for the nose
- ▶ About 100g (4oz) polyester filling
- ▶ Sewing thread to match the mohair
- ▶ Strong thread to match the mohair

FOR THE MINIATURE TEDDY

- ▶ 25 × 25cm (9 × 9in) mini-bear upholstery fabric
- ▶ Five, 9mm (⅜in) fibreboard joints
- ▶ One pair 2mm Onyx glass eyes
- ▶ 25cm (10in) no.12 black perle cotton for the nose
- ▶ 7g (¼oz) polyester filling

This miniature teddy, which stands just 9cm (3½in) high, is the perfect companion for Bedtime Georgie.

1 ▶ Make Georgie bear using the patterns on pages 66–68 and following the step-by-step bear-making guide on pages 13–19. All the dressmaking terms or procedures used to make the clothes are explained on pages 20–29. All of the bears are made from the one pattern using six different shades of mohair. These shades were created by hand dyeing (see page 127 for kit details). However, since mohair is available in so many colours, you should be able to find one that suits the clothes you have chosen for your bear.

SIX STYLES FOR GEORGIE

These easy-to-make outfits allow you to create many different looks for your Georgie. When selecting fabric for the clothes remember that Georgie is only a small bear, so avoid large prints and heavy fabrics. You will also need sewing cotton to match your chosen fabrics.

BEDTIME GEORGIE

You will need 50 x 35cm (20 x 14in) cotton print fabric for the nightshirt and 50 x 35cm (20 x 14 in) brushed-cotton print fabric for the dressing gown.

BOY IN BLUE

You will need 50 x 25cm (20 x 10in) plain cotton fabric for the dungarees and 50 x 30cm (20 x 12in) cotton print fabric for the shirt, and a 10cm (4in) Velcro fastener.

GIRL IN BLUE

Allow 50 x 20cm (20 x 8in) of cotton print fabric for the skirt, and 40 x 30cm (16 x 12in) of wool felt for the jacket. You will also need one 12mm (½in) button.

BERMUDA GEORGIE

You will need 50 x 20cm (20 x 8in) cotton print fabric for the dungarees.

DRESSED-UP GEORGIE

The frock is made from 50 x 25cm (20 x 10in) of cotton print fabric and 50 x 10cm (20 x 4in) of white cotton fabric. You will also need 70cm (28in) of 12mm wide (½in wide) lace, and a 10cm (4in) Velcro fastener.

DUFFEL-COAT GEORGIE

The duffel coat is made from 50 x 50cm (20 x 20in) of wool fabric. You will also need 50 x 50cm (20 x 20in) of lining fabric, two 12mm (½in) buttons, and 50 x 5cm (20 x 2in) of wool fabric for the scarf.

BEDTIME GEORGIE

1 For the nightshirt, trace off and cut out from your chosen fabric the front and back pattern pieces on page 90 using hem line D and sleeve length G. You will also need two front facing pieces to hem line B and a back facing (see page 25).

2 Pin the two front pieces right sides together and stitch the front seam from point A to the bottom edge. Hem the bottom edge and the sleeve edges on both the joined front piece and the back. With right sides together pin the front to the back along the shoulder

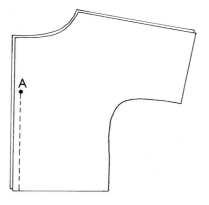

Stitch the front nightshirt pieces together from point A to the bottom edge.

and side seams. Stitch in place, then clip the seam under the arms. Turn the nightshirt right side out.

3 Stitch the front facings to the back facing at the shoulder seams with right sides together, and neaten the outer edges to prevent them from fraying. Pin the facing to the nightshirt with right sides together matching the shoulder seams and stitch in place along the neck. Trim the corners from the seam, turn the facing to the inside and press in place.

4 Cut the same pattern pieces again for the dressing gown, only this time use hem line E and sleeve length H, and follow the curved edge at the front neck opening. If you wish to add a patch pocket you will also need to cut one of the pieces marked 'bib and patch pocket' on page 89. To help you centralise the pattern of your fabric, the template has a square cut out of the middle. You can then hold this over your fabric and position a motif in the centre.

5 Hem the sleeves on the front and back pieces. With right sides together, pin the two fronts to the back along the shoulder and side seams. Stitch in place, then clip the curved underarm seam.

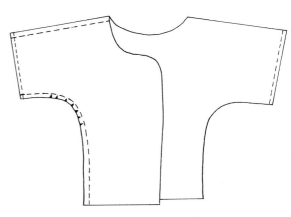

Stitch the dressing gown front to the back at the shoulder and side seams.

6 Pin the front facings to the back facing at the shoulder seams right sides together and stitch in place. Neaten the outer edge to prevent it from fraying. Place the facing onto the dressing gown with right sides together matching the shoulder seams and stitch in place along the front and neck edges. Turn right side out and create the 'shawl' collar by pressing the front neck edge to the outside as shown in the photograph. Hem the bottom of the dressing gown (see page 26).

7 Press under the seam allowance around all four sides on the patch pocket and edge stitch (see page 23) along one side only to make the top of the pocket. Tack the pocket in position and when you are happy with the way it looks, stitch in place around the remaining three sides.

MAKING THE MINIATURE BEAR

Bedtime Georgie would not be complete without his own teddy. This little bear is fully jointed and is made in the same way as the larger bears (see pages 6–19) using the pattern pieces on page 68. This bear, however, has no paw pads or foot pads. You will find it easier to sew this miniature bear by hand.

1 First oversew the pieces together to hold them in place, then stitch using reverse running stitch or backstitch (see page 23) and taking the smallest stitches you can. To make each leg, fold the leg piece in half lengthways pile sides together and stitch all around the edge leaving just the gap at the front of the leg for turning. Make the arms in exactly the same way. Place the two body pieces pile sides together and sew round the edge leaving the opening for turning. See page 10 for which stuffing to use.

Stitch the miniature bear together by hand.

2 Make the head and assemble the joints in the same way as for the larger bears, however the eyes are attached differently. These are small glass beads. When the head is complete, thread a needle with extra-strong thread long enough to pass through the head comfortably (about 25cm). Insert the needle into the back of the head, centrally at the base and as close to the joint as possible. Keeping it close to the base of the head will ensure that the knot won't be visible when the bear is completed. Bring the needle back out at the front of the head where you want the eye to go. Pull the thread through leaving a long tail of thread at the back of the head. From the front, thread a bead eye onto the needle (you may need to change to a beading needle if the hole in the bead is too small for your needle to pass through it). Slip the bead over the thread then push the needle back into the head at the same point it emerged, and bring it out next to the thread tail at the back. Remove the needle and pull the thread ends tightly together to bring the bead eye into position. Knot the thread ends together while keeping them pulled as tightly as possible. Fit the second eye in exactly the same way checking that the eyes are evenly spaced and level.

BOY IN BLUE

1 Trace off and cut out the front and back shirt pattern pieces on page 90 using hem line C and sleeve level G, and a collar piece from page 89.

2 Press under the seam allowance to the wrong side along one long edge of the collar. Fold the collar right sides together along the centre fold line marked on the pattern (the two long edges will not line up because the seam allowance has been pressed under). Stitch the short edges together at either end of the collar, trim the corners of the seam, turn right side out and press.

3 Hem the sleeves on the front and back pieces, then with right sides together pin the fronts to the back along the shoulder and side seams. Stitch in place and clip the curved underarm seam. Press under a 12mm (½in) hem to the wrong side down the front edges of the shirt and edge stitch in place.

4 Pin the collar to the neck edge of the shirt with right sides together matching the raw edges and lining up the edge of the collar with the front edge of the shirt. Stitch the collar in place and press the seam up towards the collar. Bring the pressed edge of the collar to the wrong side so that it lies on top of the seam stitching. Slipstitch (page 26) the collar in place enclosing the raw edges of the seam.

5 Hem the bottom of the shirt and stitch the Velcro fastener in place along the front opening.

6 Trace off and cut out two trouser pieces from the pattern on page 88 using the solid hem line, and two straps for the dungarees from page 89. Hem the top and bottom edges on both pieces. Pin the two trouser pieces right sides together and stitch around the curved seams only. Bring these seams together, still

Bring the stitched curved seams together to form the trouser legs and stitch in place.

with the fabric right sides facing so that the two legs are formed, and stitch in place. Clip the seam around the curved edges to allow it to spread without straining the stitching. Turn right side out and press.

7 The straps are too narrow to stitch them on the wrong side and turn them. Instead press under the seam allowance to the wrong side on each strap along both long edges. Bring the two long edges of the straps wrong sides together enclosing the pressed edges. Edge stitch in place (see page 23).

8 Put the dungarees and straps on the bear and tuck the raw edges of the straps into the waist of the trousers. Hand stitch the straps to the waistband at the front of the dungarees, then cross the straps over at the back, and hand stitch them in place. If preferred, attach the straps with press-studs – these will make it easier to remove the dungarees.

GIRL IN BLUE

1 Trace off and cut out the skirt using hem line B, the waistband and two straps from the pattern pieces on pages 87–89.
    Make up the straps for the dress in the same way as described for the boy in blue above.

2 Hem one of the long edges of the skirt (this is now the bottom edge). With right sides facing, fold the skirt in half so that the two short edges meet and stitch together from the dot marked on the pattern to

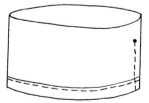

Fold the skirt in half and stitch from the marked dot to the bottom edge only.

The style and colour of the outfit you choose to dress your bear in will help to create its own special character, as these six very different Georgies show.

the bottom edge only. Press this seam open as well as the remaining seam allowance above to the waistline. Turn the skirt right side out and make two rows of gathering stitch along the top edge.

3 Fold the waistband in half lengthways and press in position. Press under the seam allowance to the wrong side along one of the long edges and stitch together along the two short edges. Turn and press.

4 Pin the raw edge of the waistband to the top edge of the skirt with right sides together and gathering up the skirt to fit the waistband. Line up one edge of the waistband to the pressed opening edge of the skirt and gather the skirt so that the waistband extends beyond the other side by 12mm (½in). Stitch the waistband in place and press the seam up towards the waistband. Bring the folded edge of the waistband to the wrong side so that the crease lies on top of the stitching and encloses the raw edges of the seam. Slipstitch (see page 26) the waistband in place.

5 Make a buttonhole (see page 28) in the extension of the waistband and sew a button on in the corresponding position. Add the straps to the skirt in the same way as described for Georgie boy in blue.

6 The jacket is made from felt and must be the simplest of Georgie's outfits to make. Cut out the front and back pieces from the pattern on page 90 using hem line C and sleeve length H. As felt does not fray, there is no need to neaten the raw edges or to add facings and hems. Pin the two fronts to the back at the shoulder and side seams and stitch in place. Turn the jacket right side out and trim the bottom edge of the sleeves and the jacket to make them perfectly level.

7 For extra detail, add buttons and patch pockets or blanket stitch around the edges of the jacket in a contrasting thread.

BERMUDA GEORGIE

1 Trace off and cut out two trouser pieces from the patterns on page 88 using the dotted line for the hem line, also two bib and patch pocket pieces, and two straps cut to the shorter dotted line from page 89.

2 Make the trousers and straps in exactly the same way as for Georgie boy in blue (except this time the trouser legs are shorter).

3 Pin the finished straps onto one of the bib pieces with right sides together making the straps sit just inside the seam allowance at each side and lining up the raw edges at the top. Tack (baste) the straps in place and remove the pins. Place the other bib piece on top with right sides facing so that the straps are sandwiched between the two pieces. Carefully stitch around the bib leaving the bottom edge open for turning. Take care that the straps do not catch in the side seams.

4 Turn the bib right way out and press. Press under the seam allowance on the bottom edge and slipstitch together to neaten. Hand stitch the bib centrally to the front of the dungarees. Put the dungarees on the bear, cross over the straps at the back and hand stitch them in place. Make sure that they are not pulled too tight or you won't be able to take the dungarees off again.

DRESSED-UP GEORGIE

1 This dress has a lace-trimmed white petticoat under a two-piece patterned skirt and lace-trimmed sleeves. Cut out the petticoat from the skirt pattern piece on page 87 using hem line C and laying the pattern on the fold as directed. Cut two skirt pattern pieces to hem line A for the outer skirt, but this time cut along the fold line shown on the pattern. You will also need front and back pieces from page 90 cut to hem line B and sleeve length F.

2 With right sides together pin the lace to the bottom edge of the petticoat and to the sleeve edges of the bodice. Edge stitch (see page 23) the lace in position and press the seam away from the lace.

3 Neaten the openings on both front pieces by pressing under 1cm (½in) to the wrong side and edge stitching them in place. Pin the two fronts to the back right sides together at the shoulder and side seams, checking that the lace on the sleeve edges lines up, and stitch together. Press under the seam allowance around the neck edge to the wrong side and edge stitch in place. Turn right side out and press. Overlap the front openings by 1cm (½in) and tack together at the bottom edge ready to be stitched to the skirt. The front opening will become the back opening when the skirt is attached.

4 With right sides together fold the petticoat so that the two short edges meet and stitch this short seam from top to bottom. Turn right side out and press the petticoat so that this seam is centre back.

5 Press under the seam allowances to the wrong side along one long edge and the two short edges of each skirt panel. Edge stitch these neatly in place. With the petticoat right side out and the front uppermost, centrally place one of the overskirt panels on top matching the raw edges at the top. Tack (baste) in position, then attach the other panel to the back of the petticoat in the same way. Make two rows of gathering stitches along the top edge and gather the completed skirt to fit the bodice.

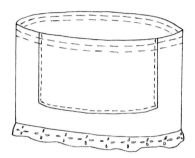

Tack the overskirt panels in position and make two rows of gathering stitches along the top edge.

6 With right sides together, pin the skirt to the bodice matching the centre back seam with the opening on the bodice and stitch in place. Stitch the Velcro fastener to the opening (page 28) to finish.

DUFFEL-COAT GEORGIE

1 This lined coat is quite easy to make. Using the patterns on pages 87–90, cut two fronts and one back to hem line D and sleeve length H, plus a hood, a scarf and two patch pocket pieces from your chosen coat fabric. Cut out the fronts, back and hood from the lining fabric as well.

2 Pin the two hood pieces right sides together along the curved edge and stitch. Do not turn right side out. Repeat this with the lining hood but turn this one right side out. Tuck the lining hood inside the fabric hood so that they are right sides together matching up the corners and raw edges, and pin in place. Stitch together around the front of the hood leaving the bottom edge open. Turn right side out tucking the lining into the hood and tack (baste) the bottom edges together to hold them in place.

3 Press under the seam allowances to the wrong side on each patch pocket. Edge stitch along the top of each pocket to neaten it. Pin them to the fronts and stitch around leaving the top edge open. Press under the hem on the sleeves to the wrong side. With right

sides together pin the fronts to the back along the shoulder and side seams. Stitch in place but do not turn right side out. Repeat all of this with the lining and this time turn right side out.

4 Tack the hood centrally to the neck edge of the coat with the right side of the hood facing the right side of the coat. Again with right sides together, pin the lining to the coat around all four edges so that the

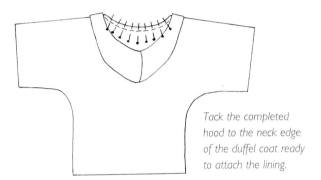

Tack the completed hood to the neck edge of the duffel coat ready to attach the lining.

hood is sandwiched in the middle. Tuck the arms of the lining into the arms of the coat to keep them safely out of the way of the seams. Stitch the lining in place leaving a gap in the bottom edge for turning the coat. Trim the corners of the seams and pull the arms of the coat out so that you can slipstitch the pressed edges of the lining to the sleeve from the inside. Turn the coat the right way out.

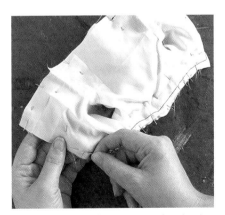

Stitch the lining to the coat around each edge

5 Finally, make two buttonholes on one side of the front opening and sew on buttons in the corresponding position on the other side.

6 Make the scarf from wool fabric fraying the ends for about 2cm (¾in). Apply a fabric fixative along the edges to prevent the scarf from fraying further.

HUGO

········· Height: 38cm (15in) ·········

Hugo and his sister Poppy are keen on walking, picnics and the outdoor life. Dressed in practical lederhosen made from suedette and a crisp white shirt trimmed with embroidered ribbon, Hugo looks as if he is about to set off on a long hike over the hills. He is also carrying a rucksack on his back – no doubt filled with chocolate and other goodies to keep him going during the day.

Hugo is made from a gorgeous two-tone mohair fabric that is trimmed around the muzzle to reveal the darker colour underneath. This subtle colouring and the solid black glass eyes make Hugo a most lovable bear.

TO MAKE HUGO

- 50 × 137cm (20 × 54in), 12mm (½in) pile German Sparse two-tone wavy-pile beige mist mohair fabric
- Five, 50mm (2in) traditional wooden or safety joints
- One pair, 11mm solid black glass eyes
- 25 × 25cm (10 × 10in) suedette for the paws
- 3m (3¼yds) dark brown perle cotton for the nose
- About 500g (1lb) polyester filling
- Sewing thread to match the mohair
- Strong thread to match the mohair

FOR HUGO'S CLOTHES

- 50 × 110cm (20 × 44in) white cotton fabric (for the shirt)
- 60cm (24in) of 25mm (1in) wide embroidered ribbon
- 15cm (6in) Velcro fastener
- 60 × 50cm (24 × 20in) suedette (for the lederhosen)
- Six, 18mm (¾in) buttons
- Four press studs
- 30 × 30cm (12 × 12in) suedette (for the rucksack)
- One, 36mm (1½in) toggle button
- 10cm (4in) leather thong
- Sewing threads to match the fabrics

Poppy and Hugo are both made from the same pattern, except that Poppy has an open, smiling mouth (see page 42 for details).

1 Make Hugo using the patterns on pages 68–73 and following the step-by-step bear-making guide on pages 6-19. The dressmaking procedures used to make the clothes are explained on pages 20–29.

2 Trace off the pattern pieces for Hugo's shirt from pages 91–94 and cut them out from your chosen fabric. Pin the two front pieces to the back with right sides together at the shoulder and side seams. Stitch in place and turn right side out. Fold the collar in half lengthways with right sides together, stitch the two short edges and turn the collar right side out again. Pin the collar to the neck edge of the shirt with right sides together and matching the centre back of the collar to the centre back of the shirt. Tack the collar in place.

3 Pin the front facings to the back facing right sides together at the shoulder seams and stitch. Pin the neatened facing (see page 25) to the shirt right sides together and stitch down the front opening and

around the neck. Press the facing to the inside and secure it to the shoulder seam with a few stitches if required. Hem the sleeves and the bottom of the shirt.

4 Stitch Velcro to the front openings for the closure then carefully sew on the embroidered ribbon trim along the top front opening and along the bottom of the sleeves, carefully matching the edges. Turn under the raw edges of the trim before stitching to neaten.

MAKING THE LEDERHOSEN

1 Trace off the pattern pieces for the lederhosen from pages 91–92 and cut them out. Hem the top and bottom edges of both trouser pieces. Pin the two pieces right sides together around the two curved seams and stitch. Bring these seams together, still with the fabric right sides together, so that two legs are formed and stitch in place (see diagram on page 34). Clip the seam around the curved edge to allow it to spread without straining the stitching. Turn and press.

The straps on Hugo's lederhosen can be crossed over at the back.

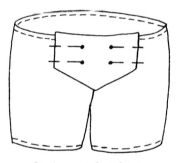

Pin the mock front flap to the lederhosen trousers.

2 Press under to the wrong side each edge of the mock front flap. Pin the flap to the trousers matching the centre of the flap to the centre seam of the trousers. Edge stitch (see page 23) the flap in place.

3 Press under the seam allowance to the wrong side along all four edges on both straps. Fold each strap in half lengthways with wrong sides facing and press. Edge stitch all around the strap.

4 Place the two bib pieces right sides together and stitch leaving a small opening at the top straight edge for turning. Turn the bib right side out, press and slipstitch (see page 26) the opening together.

5 Put the trousers on Hugo and pin the straps in place, crossing them over at the back if you wish. Pin the bib onto the straps in the desired location

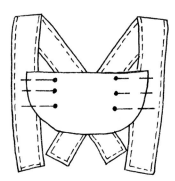

Pin the lederhosen bib to the straps and edge stitch into position.

then remove the straps from the bear without disturbing the bib. Tack (baste) the bib to the straps then edge stitch around the bib securing it at the same time to the straps.

6 Attach a press stud at each end of the straps and to the top of the trousers on either side of the mock front flap for securing the straps. Sew on the buttons: one at each end of the straps and two more in the top corners of the front flap.

MAKING THE RUCKSACK

1 Trace off and cut out the rucksack pieces using the patterns on page 95. Press under the seam allowance to the wrong side along the straight edge of the rucksack, the straight edge of the side pieces, and along all four edges of each strap. Fold each strap in half lengthways with wrong sides together and edge stitch around the four edges.

2 Pin the two side pieces to the main rucksack piece with right sides together. Match the straight edge on all three pieces, but leave this side unpinned. Fold the main rucksack piece around the sides, pin and stitch. You should now have a curved flap at the top.

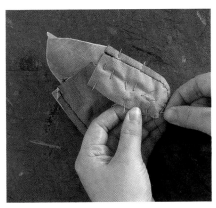

Fold the rucksack around the sides and stitch.

3 Make a loop with the leather thong and lay it in place on the right side of the curved flap with the edges slightly over the raw edge. Pin the flap facing on top with right sides together making sure the leather thong is pinned, too. Stitch in place then turn under the straight edge of the facing so that it is clear of the side pieces and stitch. Turn the rucksack the right way out.

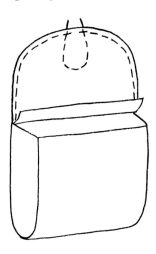

Slipstitch the front facing to the rucksack with the leather thong sandwiched between.

4 Sew a small wooden toggle in the correct position on the rucksack. Slipstitch one end of each strap to the upper back of the rucksack then attach small squares of Velcro (see page 28) to the other end of each strap and also to the lower back of the rucksack.

Hugo's rucksack is made from suedette fabric. You could also use felt.

POPPY

Poppy probably prefers a relaxing picnic to an energetic all-day hike because she is wearing a pretty summer dress and matching red sandals as shown in the photograph on page 44. She would rather settle down on the riverbank to read a book in the shade of an oak tree than scale the mountain tops like her brother Hugo. With her mouth open wide to laugh or smile, Poppy's full of fun and would make an excellent companion. Like her brother, she's practical too, and has brought her raincoat in case the weather suddenly turns bad.

TO MAKE POPPY

- ► 50 x 137cm (20 x 54in), 12mm (½in) pile German embossed oak mohair
- ► Five, 50mm (2in) traditional wooden or safety joints
- ► One pair, 14mm amber glass eyes with black pupils
- ► 25 x 25cm (10 x 10in) suedette for the paws
- ► 12 x 10cm (5 x 4in) suedette for Poppy's mouth
- ► 5 x 5cm (2 x 2in) suedette for Poppy's tongue
- ► 3m (3¼ yd) dark brown perle cotton for the nose
- ► About 500g (1lb) polyester filling
- ► Sewing thread to match the mohair
- ► Strong thread to match the mohair

FOR POPPY'S CLOTHES

- ► 50 x 110cm (20 x 44in) cotton print fabric (for the dress)
- ► 50 x 20cm (20 x 8in) white cotton fabric (for the dress apron)
- ► 80cm (31½in) of 4cm (1¼in) wide cotton broderie anglaise
- ► 40cm (16in) of 12mm (½in) wide white bias binding
- ► Three press studs or 15cm (6in) Velcro fastening
- ► 50 x 150cm (20 x 60in) red polyester lining fabric (for the raincoat)
- ► 50cm (20in) firm iron-on interfacing
- ► Three, 12mm (½in) buttons
- ► 60 x 30cm (24 x 12in) felt, red and brown (for the sandals)
- ► 60 x 30cm (24 x 12in) firm iron-on interfacing
- ► Two, decorative gold buckles
- ► 15 x 30cm (6 x 12in) stiff card
- ► All-purpose craft glue
- ► Sewing thread to match the fabrics

1 Make Poppy using the patterns on pages 68–73 and following the step-by-step bear-making guide on pages 6-19. The dressmaking procedures used to make the clothes are explained on pages 20–29.

2 If you wish to make your Poppy with a closed mouth, use the pattern for Hugo's head. For an open mouth, cut out the head, tongue and mouth patterns on page 69. Stitch the head side pieces together in the usual way, stopping at the mouth and continuing underneath it. Place the tongue centrally on top of the lower mouth piece matching the straight edges and tack in place. Place the upper mouth piece on top and stitch together along the straight back edge through all three layers. With right sides facing pin the mouth into the head matching points B, C & E on each piece.

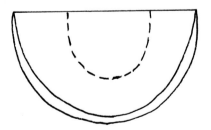

Stitch together the upper and lower felt mouth pieces with the tongue sandwiched between.

Poppy's raincoat is made from polyester lining fabric. The pattern could easily be adapted to include a hood. See Page 63.

Stitching Poppy's open mouth.

Oversew the edges together then stitch in place by hand using backstitch or reverse running stitch (see stitch diagram on page 23) taking care not to catch the tongue in the stitching. Insert the head gusset and complete the bear as described on pages 14–19.

Broderie anglaise adds the perfect finishing touch to Poppy's dress.

DRESSING POPPY

1 Trace off and cut out the pieces for Poppy's dress from your chosen material using the patterns on page 100–101. You will also need to cut a 1m x 15.5cm (1yd x 6¼in) rectangle for the skirt – a pattern piece is not included for this.

2 With right sides together pin the two bodice backs to the bodice front at the shoulder and side seams. Tack (baste) in place then stitch. Neaten the seams and press them open.

3 Neaten the opening edges of the bodice at the back then turn under and press the seam allowance to the wrong side. Edge-stitch in place.

4 With right sides together fold each piece of broderie anglaise in half so that the short edges meet and stitch along this seam. Pin these circles of broderie anglaise to the armholes of the bodice with right sides facing and matching the seam to the underarm seam of the bodice. Stitch in place.

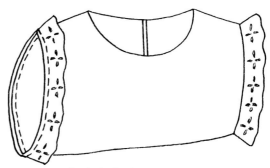

Stitch the broderie anglaise to the armholes of the bodice.

5 Pin the bias binding right sides together along the neck edge allowing it to extend past the openings by about 1cm and stitch in place. Press the bias binding away from the bodice. Turn the extended edges in to the wrong side and fold the binding to the inside of the bodice so that the folded edge lies on top of the stitching. Slipstitch this edge in position.

6 Stitch the broderie anglaise trim along one long edge of the apron with right sides together and hem the apron's two short sides. Hem one long edge of the skirt piece then fold it in half with right sides together so that the short edges meet. Stitch this seam starting from the bottom and leaving 5cm unstitched at the top. Press the seam open.

7 Matching the centre front of the apron to the centre front of the skirt, pin the apron to the skirt along the top edge with the right sides of both pieces facing up (the wrong side of the apron is facing the right side of the skirt). Tack (baste) in place. Run two rows of gathering stitch along the top edge of the

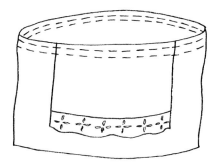

With the apron tacked in place, run two rows of gathering stitch along the top edge of the skirt.

skirt. Pull up
the gathers evenly until the skirt fits around the bottom edge of the bodice. With right sides together, pin the skirt to the bodice matching the back opening edges and stitch in place. Neaten the seam then press it up towards the bodice. Finally, add the Velcro or press-studs to the back.

MAKING POPPY'S SANDALS AND RAINCOAT

1 Cut out the sandal pieces using the patterns on page 96. Apply the firm interfacing with an iron to the wrong side of each sandal piece as well as to each strap. Fold each sandal piece in half with right sides facing so that the back edges meet and stitch in place along this short edge. Turn the sandal right side out and clip the seam allowance around the bottom at 1cm intervals.

2 Glue a main colour felt sole to one side of each cardboard sole and allow to dry. Insert this card insole into the bottom of the sandal with the felt uppermost. Push the card inside the sandal until it is level with the bottom seam allowance. Then fold the clipped edge over the card underneath. Put plenty of glue along the edge of the card and stick the bottom of the sandal to it firmly.

3 Trim the cardboard sole filler so that it fits neatly over the bottom of the sandal inside the felt edges and glue in place. Glue the dark coloured felt sole to the bottom of the sandal and allow the glue to dry

completely before finishing the sandals.

4 Make two slits in the front bar of the sandal as directed on the pattern. Pass one of the straps through these slits and position it so that it is equally spaced. Stitch one side neatly to the sandal and on the other side sew a small buckle in place. Make the other sandal in the same way, remembering to reverse the side for the buckle to make a left and a right foot. Add further trimming to the sandals if desired.

5 Poppy's raincoat is made from inexpensive lining fabric backed with firm interfacing for more rigidity. The patterns are on pages 97–99. Apply the interfacing to the wrong side of the two front pieces, the back piece and one collar piece (but not the facings). With right sides together, pin the two front pieces to the back at the shoulder and side seams and stitch in place. Clip the seams along the curved underarm seam and turn the raincoat right side out.

6 Place the two collar pieces right sides together and stitch together around the outside curved edge and short ends, leaving the inner edge open. Clip the seam at 1cm intervals and trim off the corners then turn right side out and press. Pin the collar to the neck edge of the raincoat right sides together and matching the centre back of the collar to the centre back of the raincoat. Tack the collar in place and remove the pins.

7 Stitch the front facings to the back facing at the shoulder seams then pin the neatened facing to the raincoat right sides together matching the shoulder seams. Stitch in place and press the facing to the inside. Hem the bottom edge of the raincoat and the sleeves.

8 Starting at the bottom, edge stitch neatly along one front edge, around the neck under the collar and down the other front edge. This will hold the facings in place. Edge stitch around the collar as well to add a decorative touch if desired. To finish off, add the buttons and buttonholes or Velcro with false

Poppy's sandals are made from red felt with a dark felt sole.

GRANDPA HARRY & GRANDMA HARRIET

Height: 33cm (13in) 0

Grandpa Harry and Grandma Harriet sit comfortably enjoying some well-earned rest in each other's company. Grandpa is reading the newspaper while Grandma has her knitting. Both have their spectacles, and Grandpa his comfy slippers. Don't they look contented, and perhaps a little familiar, too? What a lovely gift they'd make for any grandparents you know. Both these bears are made from the same pattern, but using two different shades of mohair fabric to give them their own special character. They are dressed in charming clothes and have jointed legs to allow them to sit in their rocking chairs. The chairs provide the special finishing touch and are easily made from plywood and painted in the colour of your choice

TO MAKE GRANDPA HARRY & GRANDMA HARRIET

- ▶ 40 × 137cm (16 × 54in) 12mm (½in) pile gold English distressed mohair fabric with black hairs (for Grandpa Harry)
- ▶ 40 × 137cm (16 × 54in) 12mm (½in) pile antique-gold plain mohair fabric (for Grandma Harriet)
- ▶ Five, 36mm (1½in) traditional wooden or safety joints
- ▶ One pair, 12mm (½in) brown glass eyes with black pupils
- ▶ 20 × 20cm (8 × 8in) wool felt for paws
- ▶ 1m, (40in) black perle cotton for the nose
- ▶ About 300 grams (12oz) polyester filling
- ▶ Sewing thread to match the mohair
- ▶ Strong thread to match the mohair

FOR GRANDPA HARRY'S CLOTHES

- 40 × 100cm (16 × 40in) white cotton fabric (for the shirt)
- 15cm (6in) Velcro fastening
- 30 × 75cm (12 × 30in) wool fabric (for the trousers)
- 50 × 20cm (20 × 8in) wool fabric (for the waistcoat)
- 50 × 20cm (20 × 8in) lining fabric
- Two, 9mm (⅜in) buttons
- 10 × 75cm (4 × 30in) wool fabric (for the slippers)
- 10 × 75cm (4 × 30in) firm iron-on interfacing
- 30 × 20 cm (12 × 8in) wool felt
- 25 × 20cm (10 × 8in) stiff card
- All-purpose craft glue
- Sewing cotton to match your chosen fabric

FOR GRANDMA HARRIET'S CLOTHES

- 60 × 110cm (24 × 44in) cotton print fabric (for the dress)
- 30 × 100cm (12 × 40in) white cotton fabric (for the apron)
- Two cocktail sticks
- Two, 5mm wooden beads
- About 5m fine knitting yarn
- Sewing cotton to match your chosen fabrics

FOR EACH ROCKING CHAIR

- 50 × 50cm (20 × 20in) 9mm (⅜in) thick plywood
- Wood glue
- A few small nails
- Fine-grade sandpaper
- Emulsion paint

1 Make Grandpa Harry and Grandma Harriet using the patterns on pages 74–76 and following the step-by-step bear-making guide on pages 6–19. All the dressmaking terms or procedures used are explained on pages 20–29.

2 These two bears have rather unique eyes: they are half covered to create eyelids. Cover half of each eye with self-adhesive paper masking tape overlapping slightly on to the back of the eye to ensure the tape is secure. Then paint each eyelid with emulsion paint and allow to dry before fitting the eyes. Omit this step if you prefer conventional eyes instead.

Grandpa's slippers are made from a wool fabric.

DRESSING GRANDPA HARRY

1 Trace off the pieces for Grandpa Harry's clothes from the patterns on pages 102–106 and cut them out from the relevant fabrics.

2 Hem the sleeves on the two shirt fronts and the shirt back. Pin the shirt fronts to the shirt back right sides together and stitch in place along the shoulder and side seams. Turn right side out.

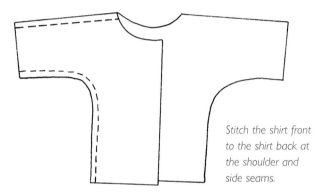

Stitch the shirt front to the shirt back at the shoulder and side seams.

Pin the front shirt facings to the back facing right sides together at the shoulder seams. Stitch in place and turn right side out. Neaten the outer edges of the facing to prevent fraying.

3 With right sides together, pin the completed facing to the shirt down the front opening and around the neck edge. Stitch in place and trim the corners from the seams to prevent the seam allowances from making a ridge on the right side of the shirt. Turn right side out and press. Finish the shirt by making a narrow hem on the bottom edge and edge stitch in place.

4 Hem the bottom and top edges of both trouser pieces. Pin the two trouser pieces right sides together and stitch around the curved seams only (see diagram on page 34). Bring these seams together, with the fabric still right sides together so that two legs are formed and stitch in place. Clip the seam around the curved edge to allow it to spread without straining the stitching. Turn right side out and press.

5 Press under the seam allowance to the wrong side around the armholes on each waistcoat piece including the lining. You will find it much easier to do this now instead of when the garment is complete. Edge stitch in place (see page 23) and clip the seams.

6 Pin the two fabric waistcoat fronts to the back right sides together at the shoulder and side seams and stitch in place. Repeat on the lining pieces. Pin the lining to the waistcoat right sides together all round the edges. Stitch in place, leaving an opening at the bottom for turning and the armholes unstitched. Turn the waistcoat and press. Slipstitch (see page 26) the waistcoat to the lining around the armholes by hand.

Slipstitch the waistcoat to the lining around the armholes by hand.

Add two buttonholes to the left side of the waistcoat (see page 28) where marked on the pattern, and two buttons in the correct positions on the right side.

7 Iron the interfacing to the wrong side of each slipper piece. Pin two of the slipper pieces right sides together and stitch along the back seam and the toe seam from the dot marked on the pattern to the

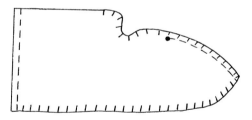

Stitch the slipper together at the heel and toe. Clip the seams along the bottom edge and around the curved seams.

bottom edge. Press the back seam open. Clip the seam allowance along the top and bottom edges of the slippers at 1cm intervals as shown, including the curved front seam. Turn the slippers right side out.

8 Glue a felt piece to one side of a card insole and allow to dry. Trim off any excess if the felt does not fit perfectly. Insert the card insole into the slipper with the felt facing inside the slipper. Push the card into the slipper until it is level with the bottom seam allowance. Fold the edge clipped earlier over the card on the underside. Put plenty of glue along the edge of

the card and stick the bottom of the slipper to it firmly. Allow the glue to dry completely. Trim the card sole filler to fit inside the fabric edge and glue in place. When this is dry, glue the felt sole in place to

Glue the clipped edge of the slippers to the sole.

cover the card and fabric edge. Trim the felt to a perfect fit when the glue is dried. Finish off the top edge of each slipper by folding the snipped seam to the inside of the slippers and gluing in place. Use glue here to reduce the chances of the fabric fraying.

9 The glasses are 'glass-less' but nevertheless very effective and easily made from soft florist's wire. This wire is readily available from garden centres and is very easy to work with. It is sometimes coated with green plastic, but this is usually only a tubing and can be removed with wire strippers before you start. Following the spectacles template on page 109, bend your wire into the correct shape and stitch securely in place on Grandpa or Grandma's nose. You may find it helpful to use a cylindrical object such as a candle or a length of round broom handle to achieve a perfect circle for each 'lens'. For a different look you can make the top of each 'lens' flat instead of round.

The spectacles are easily made from florists wire.

DRESSING GRANDMA HARRIET

1 Cut out all of the pieces for Grandma Harriet's dress using the patterns on pages 106–107. You will also need to cut out the dress skirt, the apron and apron ties from your chosen fabric, for which there are no pattern pieces. Cut a 100 x 18cm rectangle for the skirt, a 30 x 15cm rectangle for the apron and a 85 x 7cm piece for the apron ties.

2 Pin the two bodice fronts to the bodice back right sides together at the shoulder and side seams. Stitch and turn the bodice right side out. Make up the collar by pinning the two collar pieces right sides together and sewing around the outer edge. Clip the curved seam, trim off the corners and turn right side out.

3 Pin the collar to the neck edge of the bodice matching the raw edges as shown. Position the front edges of the collar 1cm (⅜in) in from the edge of the front opening to ensure it will not get caught in the seam when the facing is stitched in place. Tack (baste) the collar in place and remove the pins.

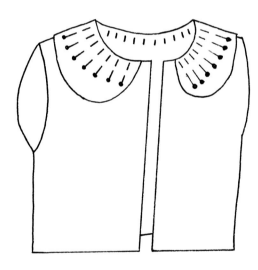
Pin the collar to the neck edge of the shirt bodice.

4 Pin the front facings to the back facing right sides together at the shoulder seams and stitch. Neaten the outer edge of the facing to prevent it from fraying. Pin the completed facings to the bodice front and neck edge with right sides together so that the collar is sandwiched between the bodice and the facing. Stitch in place along the front and neck edges, and trim to reduce the bulk of the seam.

5 Make two rows of gathering stitch along both the top and the bottom edges of each sleeve between the two sets of dots marked on the pattern (two of the dots are on the folded half of the fabric). Fold each sleeve in half lengthways with right sides together and stitch the straight underarm seam. Turn the sleeve right side out. Press under to the wrong side the seam allowance along one long edge of the sleeve band. Fold each band in half right sides together so that the two short edges meet and stitch this seam.

6 Evenly gather the bottom of each sleeve until it is the same size as the sleeve band. Pin the sleeve band to the bottom of the sleeve right sides together and matching the raw edges. Stitch in place then press the band to the inside of the sleeve so that the edge pressed earlier lies on top of the seam, encasing the raw edges. Slipstitch the sleeve band in place.

7 With right sides together, pin the sleeve to the armhole of the bodice matching the underarm seams. Gather the top of the sleeve to fit the armhole. Stitch the sleeve in place and neaten the seam. Turn the bodice right side out, overlap the front openings by 1cm and tack (baste) in place ready to fit the skirt.

8 Press under to the wrong side and edge stitch (see page 23) the hem along one long edges of the skirt. Fold the skirt in half so that the two short edges meet and stitch this back seam. Run two rows of gathering stitch along the top of the skirt and gather evenly until the skirt fits the bodice. Pin the skirt to the bodice matching the back seam of the skirt to the centre back of the bodice. Stitch the skirt in position.

Stitch the gathered skirt to the dress bodice.

9 Finish the dress either by sewing on a Velcro fastener or by making three buttonholes and attaching three buttons to the front opening of the bodice.

10 Hem the two sides and the bottom of the apron. Make the apron ties by pressing under the seam allowance along the two long sides. Fold right sides together and stitch along the short edges. Trim the corners and turn right side out. Gather the top edge of the apron so that it measures 20cm (8in). To attach the apron to the ties, place the gathered top edge of the apron centrally between the pressed edges of the ties. Tack (baste) in place making sure that the edges of the ties are level on either side of the apron. Edge stitch along the bottom of the ties, securing the apron at the same time.

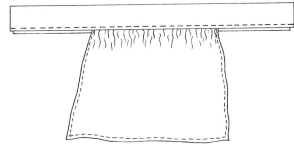

Place the top edge of the apron centrally between the ties and edge stitch in place.

11 Glue the small wooden beads to the cocktail sticks to make Grandma's knitting needles. Push them on as far as possible. Trim off the end once the glue has set and cast on a few stitches with the fine knitting yarn. You can now knit with the cocktail sticks in the normal way although it is a little fiddly at this scale. Once you have done as much knitting as you require, glue the stitches in place to make sure that they do not slip off the needles.

MAKING THE ROCKING CHAIRS

1 These chairs are very simple to make and look highly effective. Transfer the pattern shapes on pages 108–109 onto the plywood (MDF can also be used if preferred) either by tracing the outline or by gluing the pattern pieces directly onto the wood ready to cut out. If you have access to a jig saw, cutting will only take a few minutes; otherwise use a hand fret saw. This will take longer but still produce the same result.

2 First cut out the shaded areas indicated on the pattern: these are the chair sides. You will find it easier if you drill a hole large enough to thread the saw blade through at any point in the shaded area and then reconnect the blade to your saw. Now carefully

cut out the whole shaded area, just inside the line. This way your cutting does not have to be perfectly straight because afterwards you can sand the wood to the line in a smooth and neat edge. Cut out the rest of the chair pieces using the same method.

3 Start assembling the rocking chair by fixing the underseat rocker spacer centrally to the underside of the seat with glue. Leave this to set completely before going on to the next step.

4 Glue the rocker sides to either side of the rocker spacer making sure that the front of the runner is facing forward as marked on the pattern. This is very important because it balances the chair correctly when the bear sits on it. Allow to set firmly, preferably overnight, before moving on to the next stage.

5 Stand the chair upright on the rockers and glue the two sides onto the top of the seat making sure that the front and back edges are lined up. Finally, glue the back of the chair into position matching the top of the chair to the top of the sides. Insert some small nails to hold the back in place while the glue sets and to make the chair stronger. Turn the chair upside down and insert a few small nails from underneath the seat to secure the sides further. Wipe away any excess glue before it sets. Again, leave to set thoroughly and then sand the chair all over ready for painting.

6 Paint the chairs using an ordinary emulsion paint. Choose a shade to complement the bears or the room where they will be displayed. Add extra interest to your chairs by stencilling a small design or perhaps by cutting out a shape in the back or side panels of the chair with the fret saw.

Use fine knitting wool and two cocktail sticks for Grandma's knitting.

MEI YING & MEI YANG

Mei Ying and Mei Yang are two bears from different cultures. Mei Ying (opposite) is a beautiful white Japanese bear dressed in a comfortable and easy-to-make kimono secured at the waist by a wide cotton sash. Her name means 'beautiful flower' and here she is wearing a pretty garland made from ribbons and beads around her head.

In contrast, Mei Yang (see page 55) is a smart Chinese boy who is dressed in his best costume. This has a cream coloured shirt with a mandarin collar, satin trousers with a deep cuff at the ankle and a neatly shaped jacket. Both teddies are made from the same pattern but in different shades of mohair. This gives each bear its own special character.

MATERIALS FOR EACH BEAR

- ► 25 × 137cm (10 × 54in), 12mm (½in) pile antique-gold plain mohair fabric (for Mei Yang); 9mm (⅜in) pile straight natural mohair (for Mei Ying)
- ► Five, 30mm (1¼in) traditional wooden or safety joints
- ► One pair, 7mm solid black glass eyes
- ► 15 × 15cm (6 × 6in), suedette for the paws
- ► 1m (39in) black perle cotton for the nose
- ► About 250g (½lb) polyester filling
- ► Sewing thread to match the mohair
- ► Strong thread to match the mohair

1 Make Mei Ying and Mei Yang using the patterns on pages 77–79 and following the bear-making guide on pages 6–19. The dressmaking procedures used to make the clothes are explained on pages 20–29.

Mei Ying carries a pretty fan made from gift-wrapping paper.

DRESSING MEI YING

MATERIALS

- ► 60 × 110cm (24 × 44in) cotton or crepe-de-chine print fabric (for the kimono)
- ► 80 × 10cm (32 × 4in) natural white cotton fabric (for the sash)
- ► 25cm (10in) length of small white beads (cut into four separate lengths)
- ► 25cm (10in) length of 4mm wide white ribbon (cut into four separate lengths)
- ► Five, small ribbon roses
- ► 25 × 25cm (10 × 10in) suitably printed strong gift wrap paper
- ► About 5m (5½yds), silk embroidery threads (for the tassel – optional)

1 Before you can cut out the kimono pieces from your fabric you need to attach sleeves to the kimono back and front pattern pieces. Trace off the patterns on pages 110–112 and draw a second reversed sleeve. Glue the sleeves to the back and the front overlapping the edges by 6mm as a seam allowance. You also need to make a pattern for the sash measuring 80 x 10cm (32 x 4in). Now cut out these pieces from the fabric.

2 With right sides together, pin the two fronts to the back at the shoulder and side seams. Stitch along these seams and turn the garment right side out. Stitch the front facings to the back facing right sides

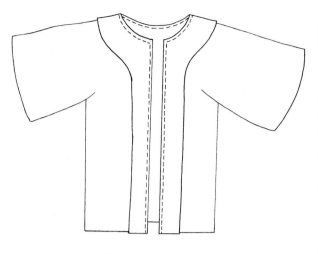

Stitch the neatened facing to the kimono.

together at the shoulder seams. Neaten the edge of the facing and pin it to the kimono matching the shoulder seams as shown. Stitch around the neck and down the front. Turn the facing to the inside and press.

Mei Ying's kimono is easily made from two pattern pieces.

3 Put the kimono onto your bear and turn up the hem so that it is level with the top of her feet. Turn under a hem on the sleeves as well, keeping them quite long but making it possible to see the bear's paws. Stitch the hems in place (see page 23).

4 Turn under the seam allowance to the wrong side on all four edges of the sash and press in position. Fold the sash in half lengthways with wrong sides together and edge stitch (see page 23) in place.

5 Hand stitch small lengths of beads and ribbon to either side of Mei Ying's head at the top of each ear. Stitch the ribbon roses to her head ensuring that you cover the ends of the beads for a neater finish.

6 To make the fan, cut a circle 18cm (7in) in diameter from the gift-wrapping paper. Fold this exactly in half with the wrong sides together to create a semi-circle with the pattern on both sides, and glue in position. When it is completely dry, fold again exactly in half to give a centre reference line then keep folding the same amount first one way, then the other, in a concertina until all of the paper has been folded. Make a tassel in the same way as for Mei Yang's hat (see page 57) and secure it to the bottom of the fan with a little glue.

DRESSING MEI YANG

MATERIALS

- 35 x 110cm (14 x 44in), cream cotton fabric (for the shirt)
- 30 x 110cm (12 x 44in) satin fabric (for the trousers and hat)
- 35 x 110cm (14 x 44in) satin fabric (for the jacket and hat)
- 10cm (4in) Velcro fastening
- About 5m (5½yds) contrasting silk embroidery threads (for the tassel)
- One press stud

1 Trace off the pattern pieces on pages 113–118 and cut out from your chosen fabric. With right sides together fold each trouser cuff in half lengthways then press under to the wrong side the seam allowance

Mei Yang is dressed in a beautiful Chinese costume with a matching jacket and tasselled hat.

along one long edge on each piece. Run two rows of gathering stitch along the bottom edge of each trouser piece and gather until it is the same length as the trouser cuffs. Pin a cuff to each leg of the trousers, matching the raw edges and stitch in place.

Stitching the cuff to one of the trouser pieces.

2 ▶ Pin the two trouser pieces right sides together and stitch around the curved seams. On one side stop at the dot marked on the pattern and turn under to the wrong side the rest of the seam allowance and stitch. Bring the curved seams together, still with right sides together, so that two legs are formed and stitch these in place. Clip the seam around the curved edge to allow it to spread easily. Fold each cuff to the inside so that the pressed edge lies over the seam and slipstitch.

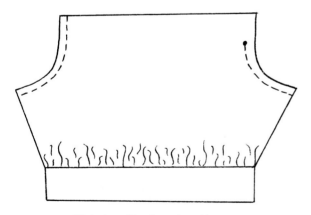

Stitch the cuff to the gathered bottom edge of the trousers before sewing them together along the curved seams.

3 ▶ Fold the waistband in half lengthways with right sides together and press under the seam allowance to the wrong side along one of the long edges. Stitch the waistband together along the two short edges only, turn right side out and press.

4 ▶ Run two rows of gathering stitch along the top edge of the trousers. Pin the waistband to the top of the trousers matching the finished edges on one side and making the waistband extend beyond the other finished edge by 3cm (1¼in). Gather the trousers

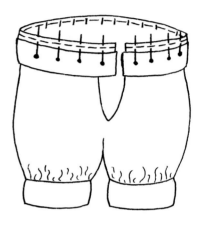

Pin the waistband to the trousers, extending one edge 3cm beyond the opening.

evenly until they fit the waistband. Stitch the waistband in place then turn the waistband to the inside of the trousers so that the pressed edge lies on top of the seam stitching. Slipstitch the waistband in place and add a button and buttonhole or Velcro for the fastening (see page 28).

5 ▶ Pin the shirt front pieces to the shirt back right sides together at the shoulder and side seams and stitch in place. Pin the two collar pieces right sides together and stitch around the curved edge leaving the bottom straight edge open. Clip the curved seam then turn and press the collar. Pin the completed collar to the neck edge of the shirt matching the centre back of the collar to the centre back of the shirt. Tack the collar in place and remove the pins.

6 ▶ With right sides together pin the two front facings to the back facing at the shoulder seams and stitch together. Turn right way out and neaten the outer edges of the facings to prevent fraying. Pin the facing to the shirt matching the shoulder seams and stitch in place through all the layers around the neck and down the front opening (see diagram on page 54). Clip the seam around the curved edge, turn and press the facing to the inside. Press the collar flat so that it stands up. Hem the bottom of the shirt and the sleeves. Attach Velcro along the front edges to close the shirt.

Mei Yang's hat is made from six pentagons of fabric.

Join up the first and last pieces on the hat.

MAKING THE JACKET AND HAT

1 Hem the bottom of the jacket sleeves: it is much easier to do this now. Pin the fronts to the back along the shoulder and side seams with right sides together and matching the finished sleeve edges. Stitch in place, clip the seams and turn the jacket right way out.

2 Pin the two curved front facings to the back neck facing at the shoulder seams with right sides together and stitch in place. Again with right sides together, pin the other back facing to the two curved front facings at the side seams and stitch in place. Make sure that the facings are not twisted before sewing them. Pin the neatened facing to the jacket edges with right sides together matching the shoulder seams as well as the side seams. Stitch in place and clip the curved edges of the seam. Press the facing to the inside and with a few small hand stitches catch it to the seams on the inside of the jacket.

3 Mei Yang's hat may look complicated but is in fact very easy to make. Cut out the hat pieces from two shades of material; three pieces from one colour and three pieces from another colour. The hat band can be made from either colour.

4 Fold the hat band right sides together so that the short edges meet and stitch these together to form a circle. Press under the seam allowance to the wrong side along one edge. Take two of the hat pieces, one of each colour, and, starting at the top point, pin them together along the side. Stitch these two in place.

Stitch two hat pieces together starting at the top.

Then pin another contrasting piece to the hat and stitch in the same way. When all six pieces have been sewn together, the first and last pieces are stitched to join up the hat.

5 Pin the hat band to the hat with right sides together matching the raw edges and the seam with one of the seams on the hat. Stitch the hat band in place then press the folded edge to the inside of the hat so that it lies on top of the seam stitches, enclosing the raw edges. Slipstitch the hat band in place.

6 Finally, make a tassel from embroidery silks in matching colours. Cut a tassel former using the pattern on page 118 and wind the lengths of embroidery silk around the card. At the top pass another thread through the loops and tie a knot to secure them, leaving one long end to attach the tassel to the hat.

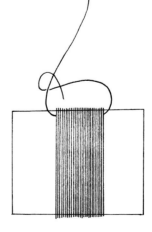

Tie the tassel together at the top to secure the threads.

Cut through the silks at the bottom to release them from the card. Holding onto the tassel, wind another thread around the tassel a little way down from the top and secure with a small knot. Use the long thread at the top of the tassel to stitch it to the top of the hat.

ANASTASIA

Height: 45cm (18in)

Anastasia is a beautiful Russian princess. She lives in the lap of luxury and her days are filled with balls, dinners and other society events. She is made from a silky long-pile mohair fabric, which adds to her exotic appeal. She is dressed in two glamorous outfits that reflect her opulent lifestyle. There's a stunning purple ballgown made from satin and lurex fabrics, and a velvet cloak trimmed with fancy buttons and a silver chain. She also has an elegant fur coat with a hat and muff to match that are ideal for a cold Russian winter. No expense is spared when it comes to making this large and beautiful bear – but the result is well worth it.

TO MAKE ANASTASIA

- 60 × 137cm (24 × 54in), 25mm (1in) pile German Buttermilk Wave mohair
- Five, 64mm (2½in) traditional wooden or safety joints
- One pair, 16mm blue glass eyes with black pupils
- 20 × 25cm (8 × 10in) suedette for the paws
- 3m (3¼yds) dark brown perle cotton for the nose
- About 800g (2lb) polyester filling
- Sewing thread to match the mohair
- Strong thread to match the mohair

FOR ANASTASIA'S CLOTHES

- 75 × 110 cm (30 × 44in) satin fabric (for the ballgown)
- 50 × 110cm (20 × 44in) Lurex fabric (for the ballgown)
- 15cm (6in) Velcro fastening
- 90 × 110cm (36 × 44in) velvet fabric (for the cloak)
- 80 × 110cm (32 × 44in) lining fabric
- Two, 25mm (1in) fancy buttons
- Two, 8cm (3in) lengths of silver chain
- One small clasp
- 50cm (20in) jewelled braid
- Sewing cotton to match your chosen fabrics
- One small tiara, available from toy shops

Make a drawstring bag for Anastasia using leftover fabric from the cloak.

1▶ Make Anastasia bear using the patterns on pages 80–86 and following the step-by-step bear-making guide on pages 6–19. Take extra care when cutting out the pattern pieces on such a long-pile fabric to avoid cutting through the fur pile as well as the backing. All the dressmaking terms or procedures used to make the clothes are explained in the step-by-step guide on pages 20–29. We used a Lurex fabric for the ballgown bodice and black satin for the skirt, but there are many other wonderful fabrics to choose from.

2▶ Trace off the pattern pieces for the ballgown on pages 119–121 and cut them out from your two fabrics. Pin the two bodice backs to the bodice front at the shoulder and side seams with right sides together and stitch in place. Neaten the seams and press.

3▶ Neaten both openings on the back by pressing under a 15mm (½in) hem to the wrong side. Edge stitch (see page 23) in place. Neaten the neck edge with bias binding. You can either make your own (see page 27) or use ready-made binding. Fold the binding over the raw edge and sew in place. Overlap the opening edges at the bottom of the bodice so that the hems match and tack (baste) in place ready to attach the skirt.

4▶ With right sides facing pin the satin underskirt front and back pieces together along the side seams and tack (baste) in place. Stitch along these seams, neaten the raw edges to stop fraying and press. Repeat the same procedure with the Lurex overskirt, then turn both skirts right way out. Lay the Lurex overskirt

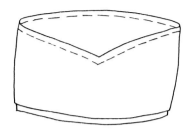

Tack the over-skirt in position, matching the centre fronts.

over the satin underskirt, matching the centre front and the side seams. Tack in place around the top edge.

5 Run two rows of straight gathering stitch along the top of the skirt, the first on the seam line and the second slightly inside. Pull up the gathers evenly until the skirt fits around the bottom of the bodice. Pin the skirt to the bodice with right sides together and matching the side seams and the centre front points. Stitch the skirt in place, neaten the raw edges and press the seam up towards the bodice. Hem the bottom of both the underskirt and the overskirt, making the overskirt slightly longer.

6 Fold each sleeve piece in half lengthways and stitch together along the straight underarm seam. Place each Lurex sleeve over a satin sleeve, match the underarm seams and tack (baste) together to hold in place. Run two lines of gathering stitch along both the top and the bottom of the sleeve between the two sets of dots marked on the pattern (note: the second dot in each set is on the folded fabric).

7 Fold under the seam allowance to the wrong side along one long edge of each sleeve band and press. Fold the band in half so that the two short edges meet and stitch along this seam. Pull up the gathers evenly along the bottom of the sleeve until this is the same size as the sleeve band. With right sides together, pin the band to the sleeve, matching the raw edges. Stitch together then press the sleeve band to the wrong side so that the crease you made earlier lies on top of the seam you have just sewn, and encases the raw edges of the seam. Slipstitch (see page 26) the sleeve band in place.

Slipstitch the sleeve band in place to the wrong side of the sleeve.

8 Insert the completed sleeves into the dress. With right sides together, match the underarm seams on the sleeve and the dress, and pin the sleeve in position. Gather the top of the sleeve evenly to fit the opening and tack (baste) the sleeve in place. Stitch in position and neaten the seams to finish.

9 Trim the Velcro to make a thin band if necessary and stitch the closure in place (see page 28).

MAKING THE CLOAK AND BAG

1 You will only find a pattern for the cloak hood on page 123. You will also need to cut out a 110 x 45cm rectangle from the velvet and the lining fabric.

2 Make the hood by pinning the two velvet pieces right sides together along the curved edge and stitching in place. Repeat this with the two lining pieces. Attach the lining to the hood by pinning them right sides together along the front of the hood leaving the bottom edge open. Stitch in place.

Make a lining for the cloak and its hood.

3 Turn the hood right side out so that the lining sits inside the hood and press. Run two lines of gathering stitch along the bottom raw edge of the hood starting and finishing 5cm (2in) in from either edge.

4 Run two more lines of gathering stitch along the top edge of the cloak again starting and finishing 5cm (2in) in from either edge. Gather this edge evenly until the cloak measures 38cm (15in) from edge to edge along the top. Repeat this with the lining pieces.

5 Pin the hood to the cloak with right (velvet) sides together and matching both edges of the hood to the start of the gathering on the cloak. Gather the bottom of the hood to fit. Tack (baste) in place then put the gathered lining on top of the cloak right sides together with the hood sandwiched in between. Tack the lining in place around all four edges and stitch leaving a gap in the bottom seam for turning. Turn the cloak right way out, press and slipstitch the opening to finish.

6 Make the closure by sewing on the fancy buttons. Attach the chain to one button by opening one of its links with pliers, wrapping the chain around the back of the button and re-connecting the link to the chain. Repeat with the other piece of chain on the other button and attach a small clasp to one side.

7 Cut out the drawstring bag pieces from the patterns on page 121. Press under the seam allowance to the wrong side on one long edge of the drawstring bag and stitch to make a casing. Fold it in half lengthways with right sides together and stitch the side seams, leaving an opening for the braid to pass through. Press the seams flat then pin the side around the base right sides together. Stitch in place and turn. Thread the braid through the casing leaving loops at either side for the handles and secure the braid ends.

ANASTASIA'S OUTDOOR OUTFIT

You can also dress Anastasia in a sumptuous lined fur coat, hat and muff trimmed with frog fasteners and a brooch. Turn to page 5 for a photograph of this outfit.

MATERIALS
▹ 1m × 137cm (40 × 54in) fur fabric
▹ 1.5m × 110cm (60 × 44in) lining fabric
▹ Two pairs frog fasteners for the coat
▹ 75cm (30in) leather thong for the muff
▹ Sewing cotton to match

1 Trace off all the pieces for the coat, hat and muff using the patterns on page 122–126 and cut them out from the fur and lining fabrics. See page 14 for advice on cutting fur fabric.

2 With right sides together, pin the coat fronts to the back at the shoulder and side seams and stitch in place.

3 Hem the bottom of each sleeve, then fold the sleeve right sides together and stitch along the straight underarm seam. Turn the sleeves right side out and insert them into the armholes of the coat. Stitch in place. Pull the arms out so that the fur coat is the wrong way out. Make up the lining in exactly the same way.

4 Turn the lining right way out. With right sides together pin the lining to the coat around all four edges. Tuck the arms on the lining into the fur arms to keep them out of the way (they are stitched later). Stitch the lining to the coat around all four edges remembering to leave a fairly large gap for turning in the bottom seam. Trim the corners of the seams to reduce their bulk and turn the coat right side out. Pull the arms through to the wrong side, slipstitch the hemmed edges of both the fur sleeve and the lining together and turn the coat right side out.

Stitching the lining to the fur coat.

5 Put the coat on Anastasia and decide where the frog fasteners will go. Slipstitch the frogs to the coat ensuring that they are level.

6 Fold the hat band in half with right sides together so that the two short sides meet and stitch this seam. Pin the band around the top of the hat with right sides together and stitch in place.

7 Make the hat lining in the same way and turn right side out. Pin the lining to the fur hat with right sides together and stitch together around the base of the hat, leaving a gap for turning. Turn right side out and slipstitch the opening. This simple design can easily be made larger to create a different look (see Adapting the Patterns on page 62).

8 With right sides together, pin the lining to the muff along two long sides and stitch. Turn the muff right side out, then fold it in half right sides together so that two short edges meet and stitch this seam.

9 Pass the leather thong through the muff and put it onto Anastasia to measure how long it needs to be. Make a knot in the thong at the required length and twist it around so that it is hidden inside the muff.

ADAPTING PATTERNS

Teddy bears come in a great variety of sizes from short to tall and from rather plump to those who look as if they need a little more honey. You can easily create outfits for any of the bears featured in this book by following the instructions, but what do you do if you want to make a smart new set of clothes for one of your own bears?

The patterns are designed using a minimum amount of pieces. This makes their construction, and therefore any alterations, quite straightforward. Each of the patterns has adjustment lines marked on it, so you can fit the outfits to a different size bear. If you are a newcomer to making and dressing bears, it is advisable to complete a few of the outfits exactly as they appear by following the instructions before you try to alter them. That way you will have a better understanding of how these simple clothes are put together.

ALTERING A PATTERN

1 If you wish to make one of the outfits that appear in this book for your own bear and it has been designed for a smaller bear, the easiest way to scale up the pattern pieces to roughly the right size is by enlarging them on a photocopier. Once you have the new enlarged pattern, make up the outfit using an old cotton sheet or other thin firmly-woven material so that you can see where any adjustments need to be made. There is no need to sew hems as these can be cut away on this practice piece. However, do remember to include a hem allowance if you have to alter any of the pattern pieces.

2 Put the cotton outfit on your bear and have a good look to see if the clothes are too tight or too loose in any places. Teddy bears are unique in their shape and construction and you are most likely to encounter fitting problems across the back (especially if your bear has a hump) and around the arm and leg joints. Make notes as you examine your bear. What about the hemline – is it too long or too short? Is there enough room in the armholes for the arms to move freely? Are the sleeves too long or too short?

Does the garment fit across the back of the bear or does it need taking in or letting out? If the garment is generally too large it is easy to use pins to take in the excess material and transfer these differences to the pattern pieces.

3 Adjustment lines have been incorporated into the patterns on pages 87–126 to help you alter areas of a garment that may be too small for your bear. For example, if the armhole on a shirt or bodice is too tight you need to cut the pattern along this line. The pattern can then have another piece of paper inserted between the cuts to make the armhole the required depth. If you need to make the adjustment to a pattern that has separate sleeves the depth of the sleeve also needs to be altered. Cut the sleeve pattern piece in half down the centre from top to bottom and insert paper in between these cuts to make the sleeve the required depth.

4 If the back of the garment is too tight, redraw the pattern adding an extra allowance to the centre back of the garment. If you have to do this, bear in mind that the neckline will probably alter, too, and this may affect the front neckline. If this makes the neckline too low, keep a note of the measurement and redraw this part of the pattern front and any facings. If the neckline becomes too high, use a pen to draw the desired neckline onto your cotton garment then transfer this to the paper pattern remembering to add a seam allowance. You will also need to adjust collars and facings to match a new neckline.

5 The length of sleeves and hemlines can easily be adjusted: simply make a note of the amount they need to be either lengthened or shortened and transfer these measurements to the paper patterns.

6 When you have made all of the necessary adjustments on your paper patterns make up a second outfit from the cotton sheet to check that you now have a perfect fit. Then you can make up the complete outfit from your chosen material and feel confident that the garment will fit.

OTHER WAYS OF ADAPTING PATTERNS

There are many other ways you can adapt the patterns in this book to create a different garment, regardless of whether you have to adapt the fit. The simplest way to change the look of a garment is to use different fabrics. A brighter fabric with a stronger pattern will not only change the look of the garment but will also change the character of your bear.

Adding small accessories will also help to change the appearance and character of your bear. Grandpa Harry and Grandma Harriet's glasses (see page 46) will sit happily on the end of any bear's nose. Hugo's rucksack (see page 38) and Poppy's sandals (see page 42) can be scaled up or down to fit another bear, and why not give every bear a little teddy of their own like Bedtime Georgie's on page 31? You can further enhance a bear's character by buying a pair of small children's shoes or boots which would suit Hugo, or tiny wellington boots which would suit Poppy.

Simple adjustments can be made which create a completely new garment. These include shortening the trouser patterns to create shorts, adding a simple cuff to the bottom of trousers to create knickerbockers, or adding elastic to the waist and legs to make bloomers that would be especially suitable for Grandma Harriet.

Sleeves can be shortened (or lengthened) or left off altogether. Why not add an embroidered trim like the one on Poppy's dress or simple bias binding around the armhole? The methods are exactly the same for any size bear.

Collars can easily be added or omitted from any design, as can hoods on coats or cloaks. Omit the hood from Georgie's duffel coat and try your hand at designing a collar for it instead. Copy the collar shape from another garment and make it the appropriate size. Tack (baste) the collar in place along the neck edge as described for Hugo's shirt on page 40 before adding the lining as described on page 37.

Skirt lengths can easily be made longer or shorter on the paper pattern. As all of the skirts on the outfits in this book are gathered, fitting them over leg joints poses no problem. Sewn-in aprons and delicate overskirts are also easy to incorporate: simply follow the instructions for Poppy's apron on page 45 or Anastasia's overskirt on page 59, adjusting the size of the pattern to fit your bear if necessary. A beautiful wedding dress can easily be made for Anastasia with no alteration to the ballgown pattern. Instead of cutting an overskirt and sleeves from Lurex fabric, use white or ivory satin. Then cut a second set of bodice and back pieces from fine lace fabric to fit over the satin fabric and tack (baste) in place. Continue making up the dress following the instructions on page 59-60.

You can easily omit the lining from a garment if you prefer, but you will then need to make front and back facings to neaten the raw edges. This is not difficult. Lay the front and back pieces onto a large sheet of paper so that the shoulder seams are touching. Draw around the pattern from the bottom edge of the front piece, along the front opening edge, around the neck edges and a little way down the centre back line. Mark also where the shoulder line is: this will be important later. Take the original pattern pieces away and draw on your own facings. These patterns can now be cut out, separating the back facing from the front facing at the shoulder seam, and used to cut out facings from your fabric.

Once you have made a few of the featured outfits new ideas for adapting the patterns to create different outfits will easily come to mind. By using the simple pattern pieces featured here a whole new wardrobe can be created for any of your bears. Once you have a little confidence why not try designing outfits of your own? Your imagination can really run wild creating elaborate and detailed garments from the vast range of fabrics that is available. Making test garments from old cotton sheets will allow a greater freedom for designing without the worry of wasting expensive fabric. Most of all, have fun designing and making clothes for your bears as not only are you giving them a new outfit to wear, you are also creating a new character for each one.

You can easily adapt the dress patterns in this book to create a unique style for your own bear. Shown here are some alternative ways of making up the patterns. From the left, the blue corduroy trousers are simply Hugo's lederhosen without the bib. The navy blouse is made from Grandma's dress bodice, with trim around the collar. The next four items are adapted from Georgie's dress patterns: tartan fabric gives trousers a new look; leave off the pinafore straps to make a skirt; sew the skirt to the top to make the dress, adding bias binding trim; and add an eye-catching animal print fabric to the jacket's collar and pockets for a stylish twist. Second from the right, adapt Grandpa's shirt pattern to make a jacket using different fabric with added trim. To make the pretty floral dress simply lengthen Mei Yang's shirt pattern at the hem. Poppy holds Grandpa's waistcoat, cut from alternative fabric, without buttons or buttonholes, for the younger, jauntier bear. Finally, in the basket, the crisp white shirt is made from Georgie's basic pattern pieces.

BEAR PATTERNS

In this chapter you will find all the patterns you need to make the traditional teddy bears in this book. Full instructions on how to make each bear can be found in the step-by-step guide to bear-making on pages 13–19. Included in these steps is an explanation of how to use the letters, arrows and dots marked on the patterns. Then on page 87 you will find the dressmaking patterns needed to make all the outfits worn by the bears in this book. An explanation of the essential dressmaking techniques needed to make the clothes can be found on pages 20–29.

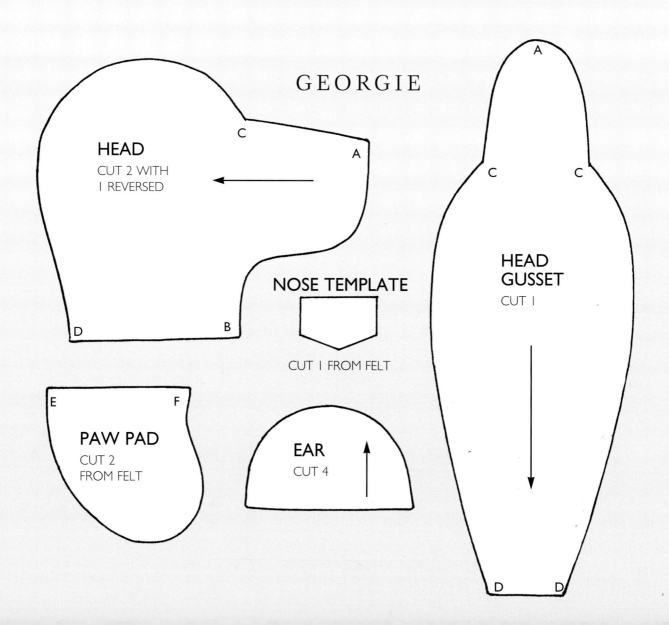

GEORGIE

HEAD
CUT 2 WITH
1 REVERSED

NOSE TEMPLATE
CUT 1 FROM FELT

HEAD GUSSET
CUT 1

PAW PAD
CUT 2
FROM FELT

EAR
CUT 4

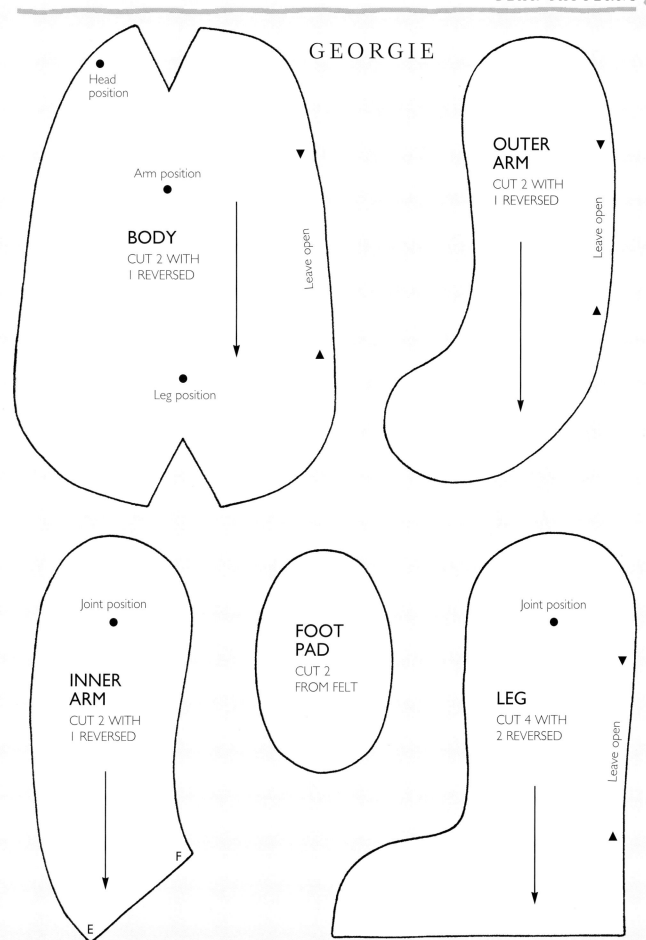

GEORGIE

Head position

Arm position

BODY
CUT 2 WITH
1 REVERSED

Leave open

Leg position

OUTER
ARM
CUT 2 WITH
1 REVERSED

Leave open

Joint position

INNER
ARM
CUT 2 WITH
1 REVERSED

F

E

FOOT
PAD
CUT 2
FROM FELT

Joint position

LEG
CUT 4 WITH
2 REVERSED

Leave open

MINIATURE TEDDY BEAR

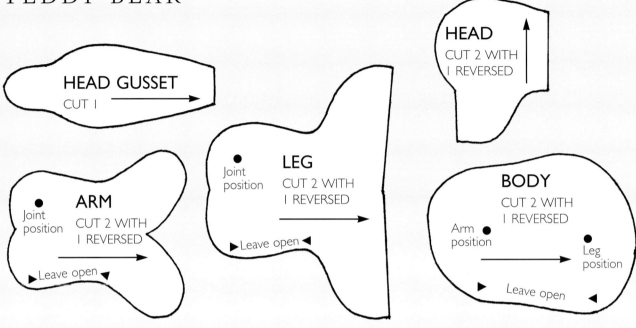

HEAD GUSSET
CUT 1

HEAD
CUT 2 WITH
1 REVERSED

ARM
CUT 2 WITH
1 REVERSED
Joint position
Leave open

LEG
CUT 2 WITH
1 REVERSED
Joint position
Leave open

BODY
CUT 2 WITH
1 REVERSED
Arm position
Leg position
Leave open

HUGO & POPPY

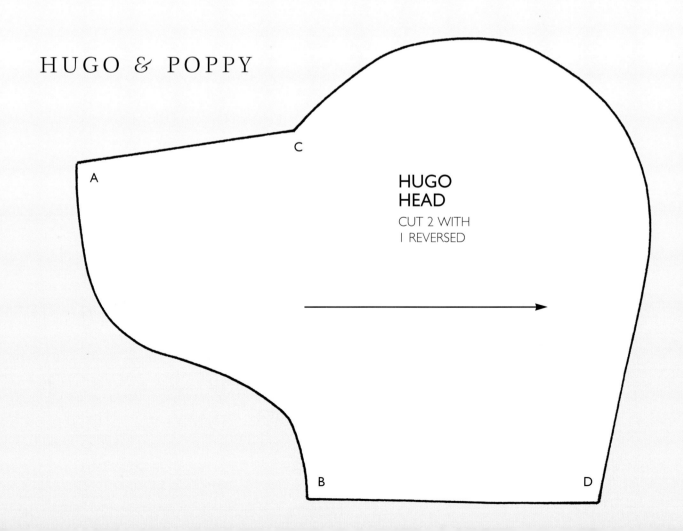

HUGO HEAD
CUT 2 WITH
1 REVERSED

A

C

B

D

HUGO & POPPY

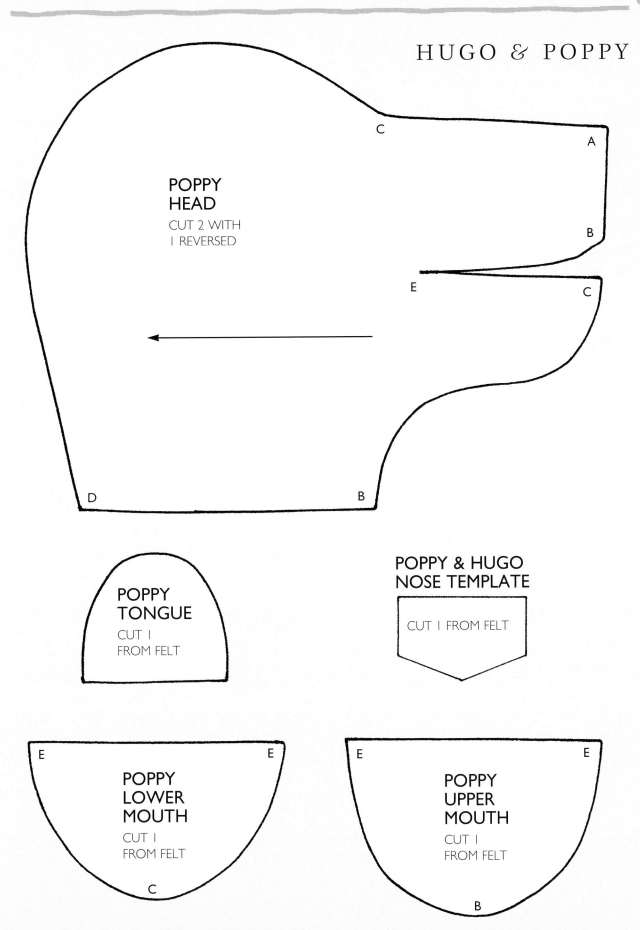

POPPY HEAD

CUT 2 WITH
1 REVERSED

C

A

B

E

C

D

B

POPPY TONGUE

CUT 1
FROM FELT

POPPY & HUGO NOSE TEMPLATE

CUT 1 FROM FELT

POPPY LOWER MOUTH

CUT 1
FROM FELT

E

E

C

POPPY UPPER MOUTH

CUT 1
FROM FELT

E

E

B

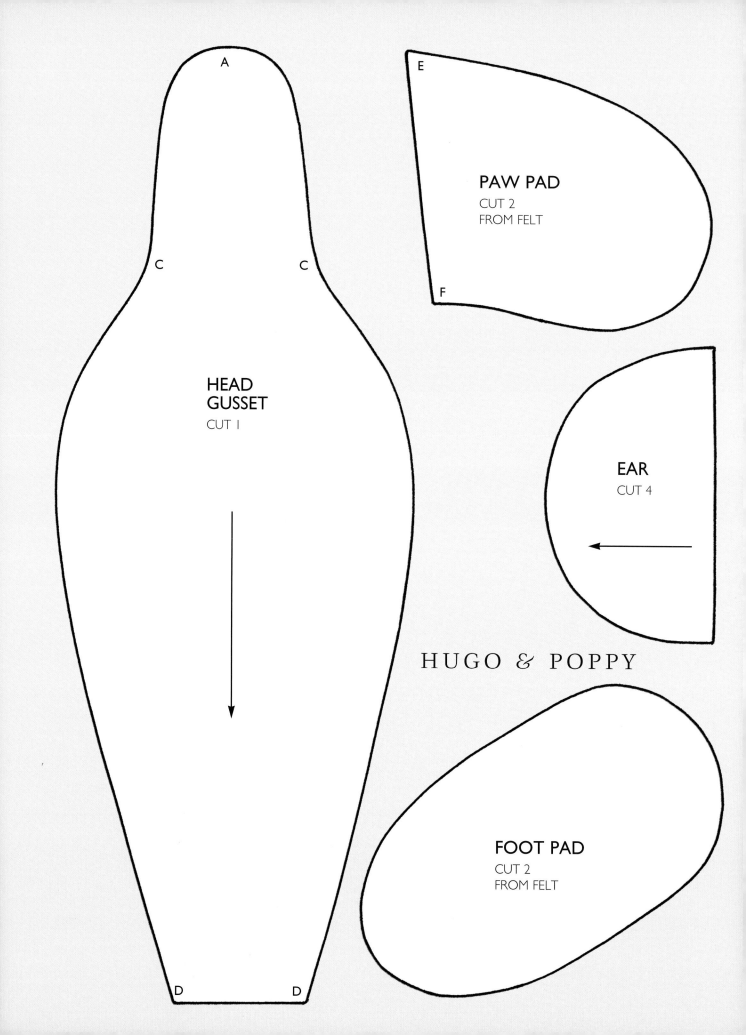

A

E

PAW PAD
CUT 2
FROM FELT

F

C   C

HEAD
GUSSET
CUT 1

EAR
CUT 4

HUGO & POPPY

FOOT PAD
CUT 2
FROM FELT

D   D

HUGO & POPPY

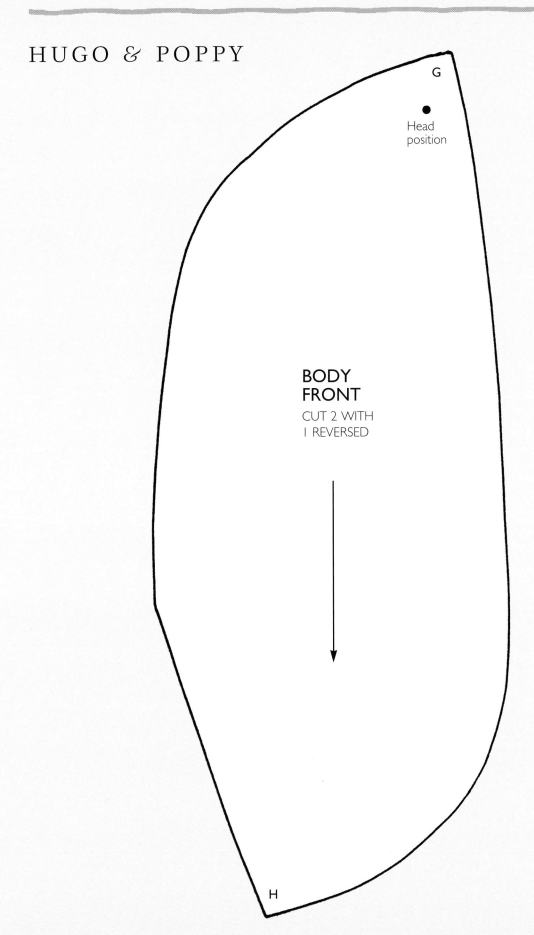

G

●
Head
position

**BODY
FRONT**

CUT 2 WITH
1 REVERSED

H

HUGO & POPPY

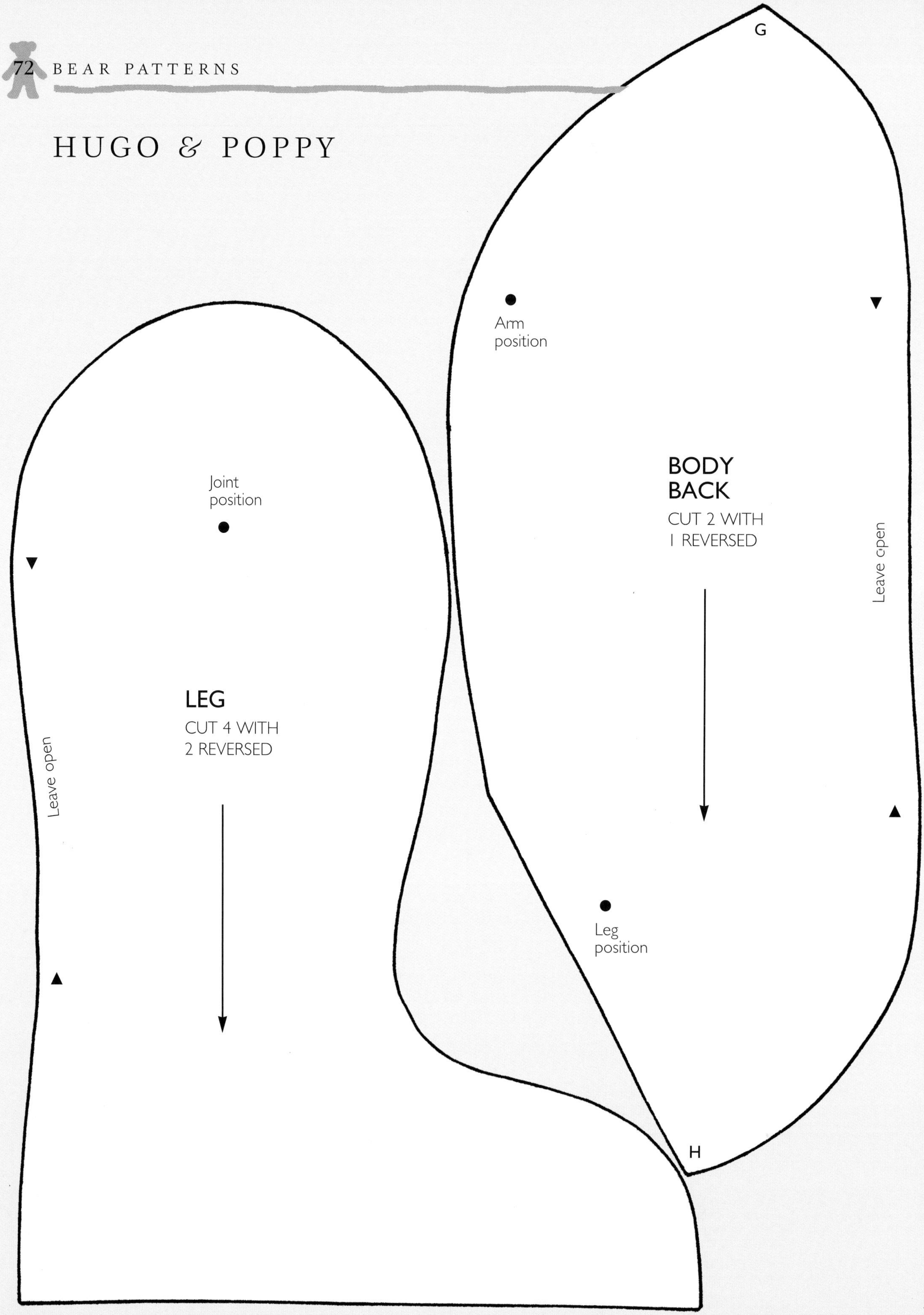

G

Arm
position

▼

BODY
BACK
CUT 2 WITH
1 REVERSED

Leave open

▲

Joint
position

▼

LEG
CUT 4 WITH
2 REVERSED

Leave open

▲

Leg
position

H

HUGO & POPPY

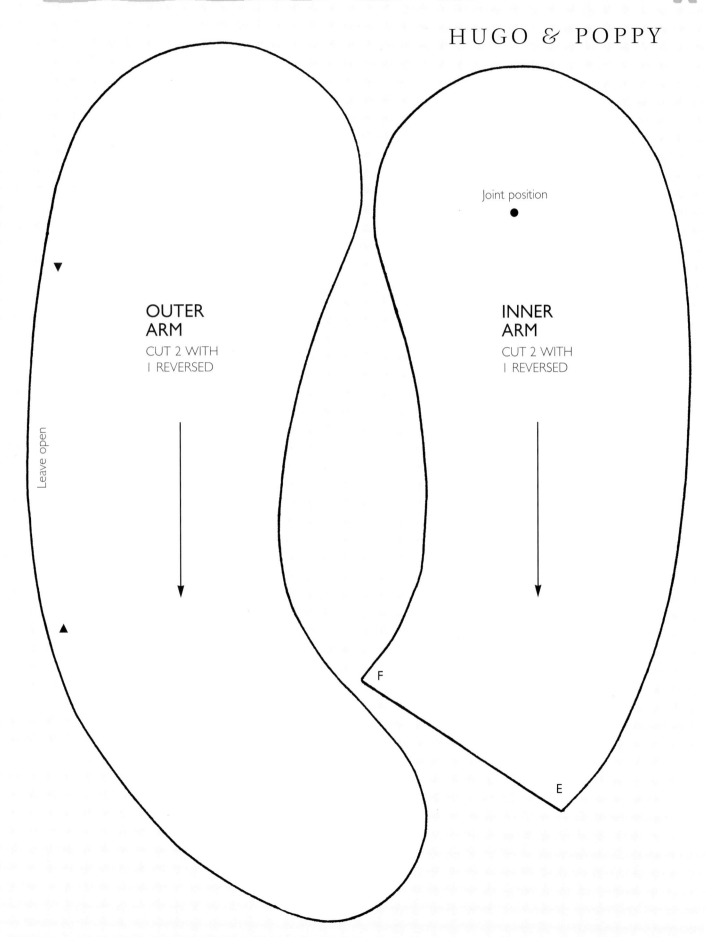

OUTER
ARM
CUT 2 WITH
1 REVERSED

Leave open

INNER
ARM
CUT 2 WITH
1 REVERSED

Joint position

F

E

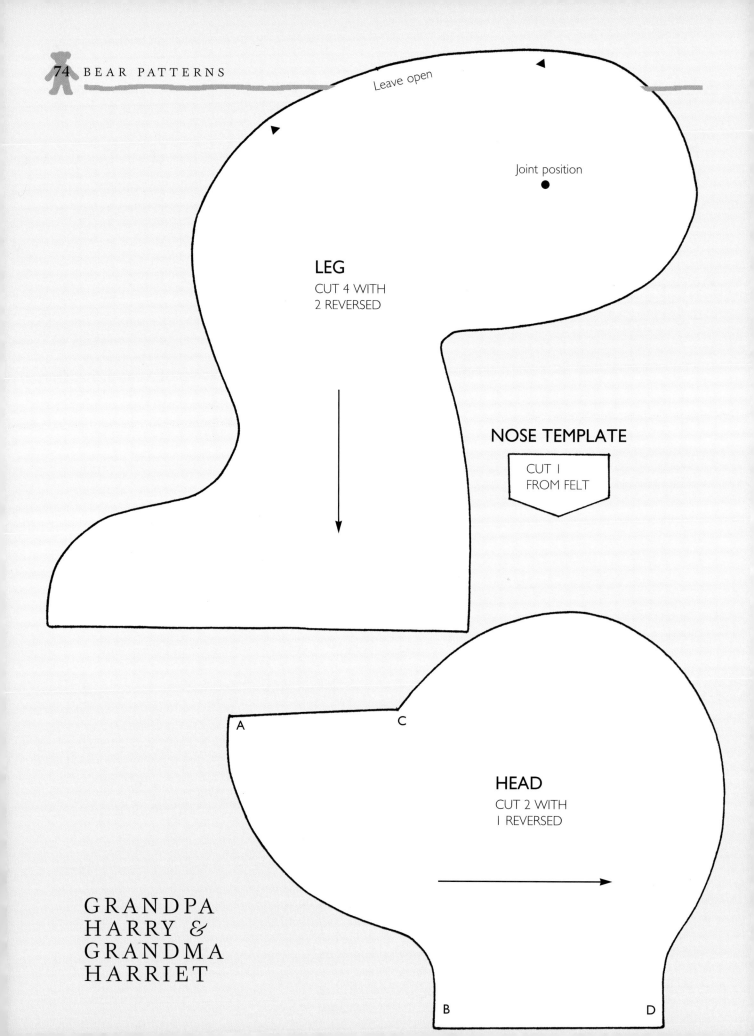

Leave open

Joint position

LEG
CUT 4 WITH
2 REVERSED

NOSE TEMPLATE

CUT 1
FROM FELT

A

C

HEAD
CUT 2 WITH
1 REVERSED

GRANDPA
HARRY &
GRANDMA
HARRIET

B

D

GRANDPA HARRY & GRANDMA HARRIET

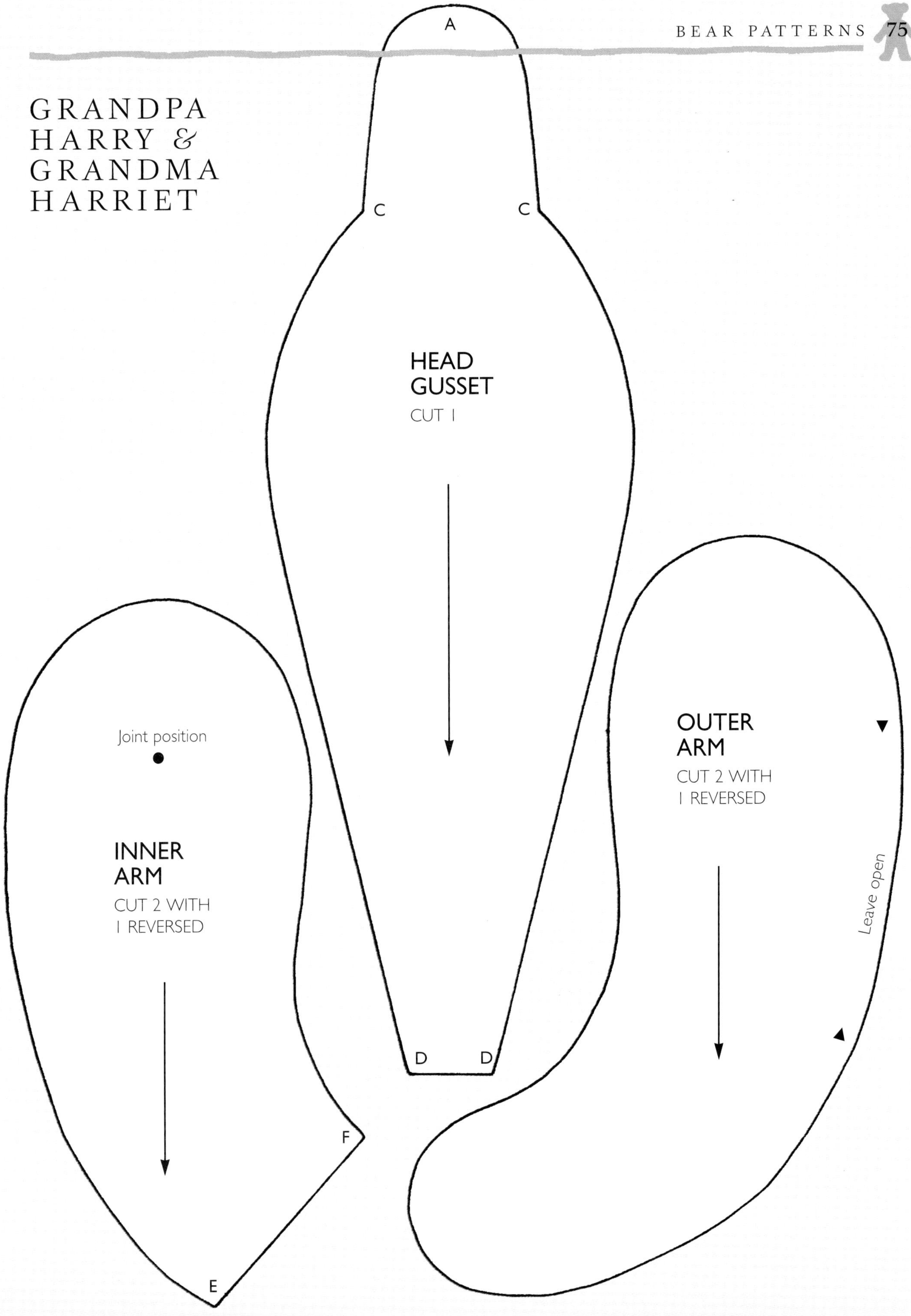

A

C   C

HEAD GUSSET

CUT I

D   D

Joint position

INNER ARM

CUT 2 WITH I REVERSED

F

E

OUTER ARM

CUT 2 WITH I REVERSED

Leave open

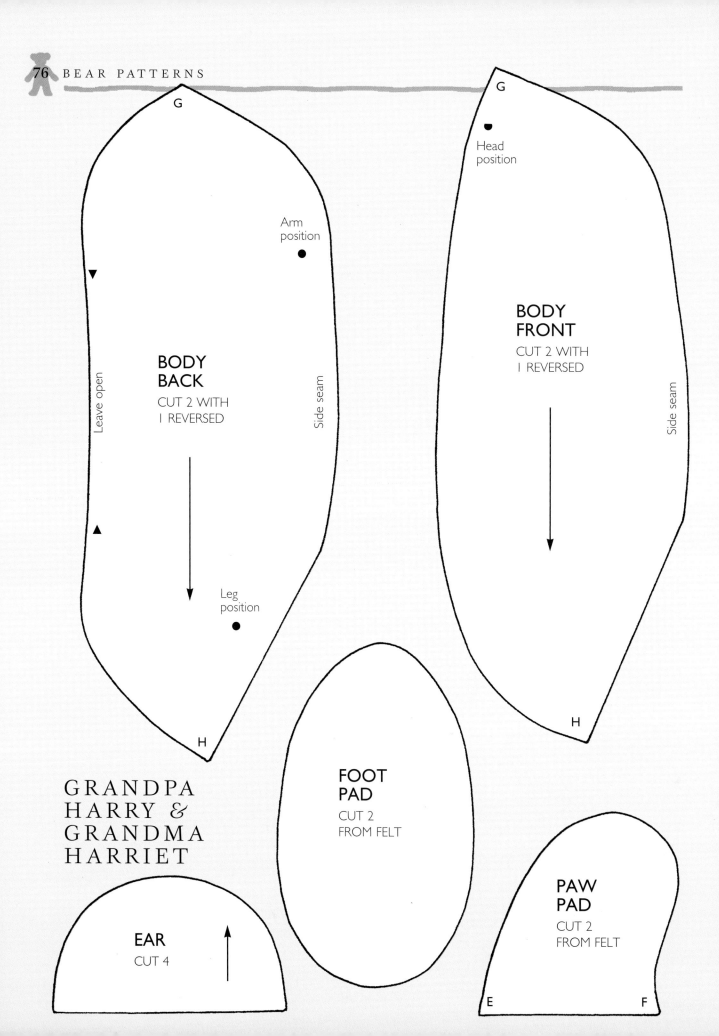

G

Arm
position

Leave open

**BODY
BACK**

CUT 2 WITH
1 REVERSED

Side seam

Leg
position

H

G

Head
position

**BODY
FRONT**

CUT 2 WITH
1 REVERSED

Side seam

H

GRANDPA
HARRY &
GRANDMA
HARRIET

**FOOT
PAD**

CUT 2
FROM FELT

**PAW
PAD**

CUT 2
FROM FELT

EAR

CUT 4

E   F

A

C   C

HEAD
GUSSET
CUT 1

D   D

A

B

C

D

HEAD
CUT 2 WITH
1 REVERSED

MEI YING &
MEI YANG

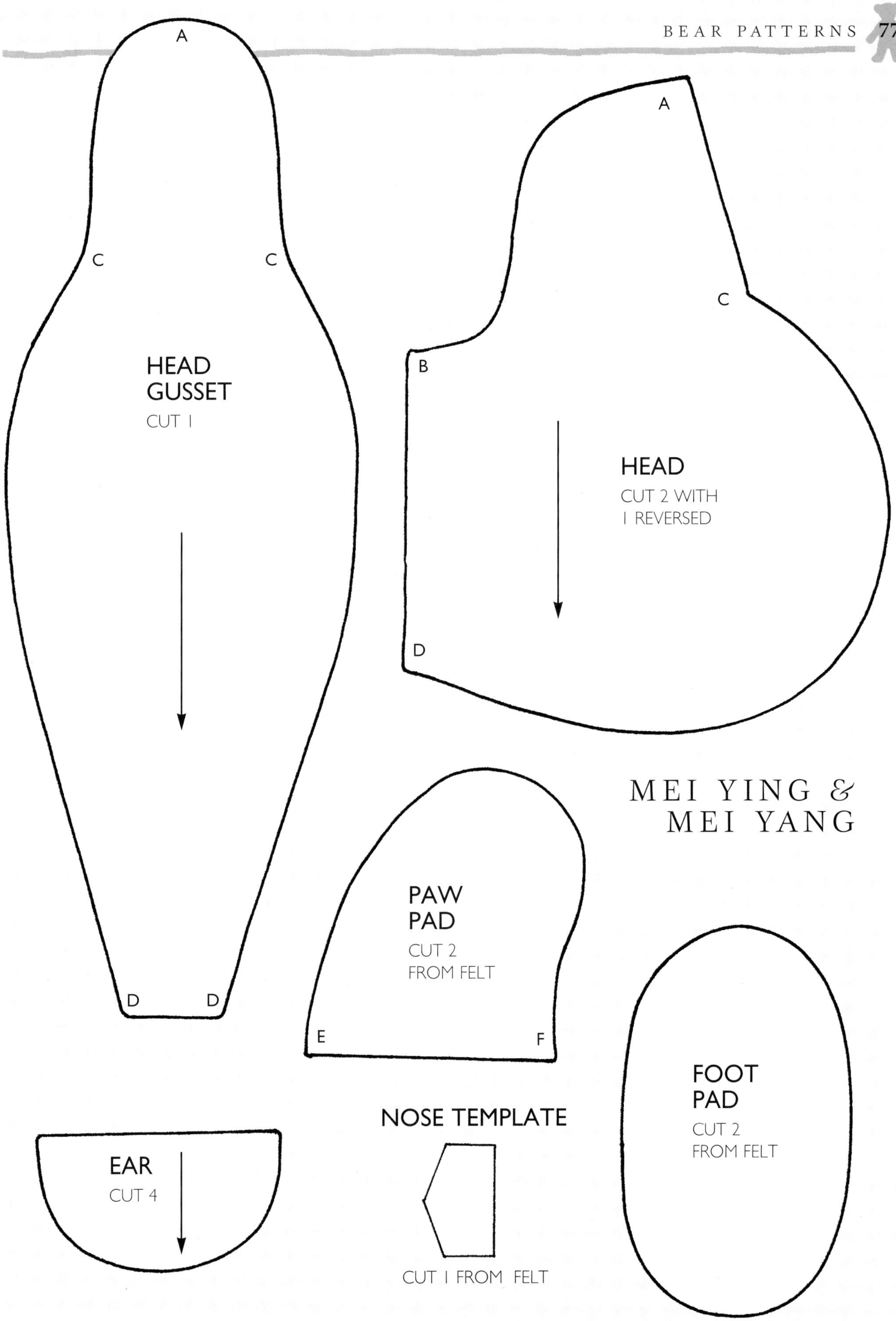

PAW
PAD
CUT 2
FROM FELT

E   F

FOOT
PAD
CUT 2
FROM FELT

EAR
CUT 4

NOSE TEMPLATE

CUT 1 FROM FELT

MEI YING &
MEI YANG

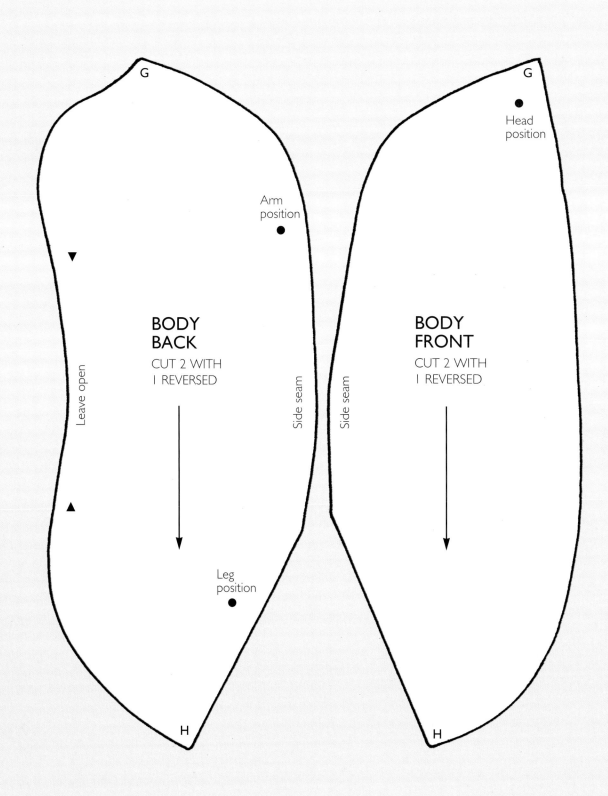

G

Arm
position

●

▼

BODY
BACK

CUT 2 WITH
1 REVERSED

Leave open

Side seam

↓

Leg
position

●

H

G

Head
position

●

Side seam

BODY
FRONT

CUT 2 WITH
1 REVERSED

↓

H

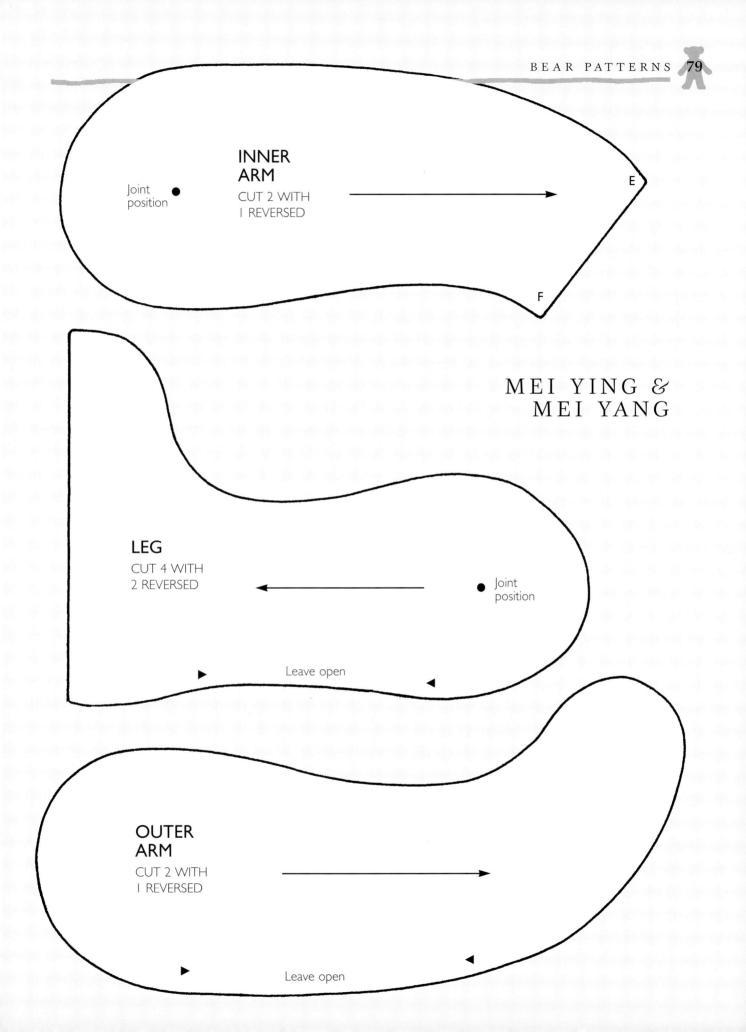

INNER ARM

CUT 2 WITH
1 REVERSED

Joint position

E

F

MEI YING &
MEI YANG

LEG

CUT 4 WITH
2 REVERSED

Joint position

Leave open

OUTER ARM

CUT 2 WITH
1 REVERSED

Leave open

ANASTASIA

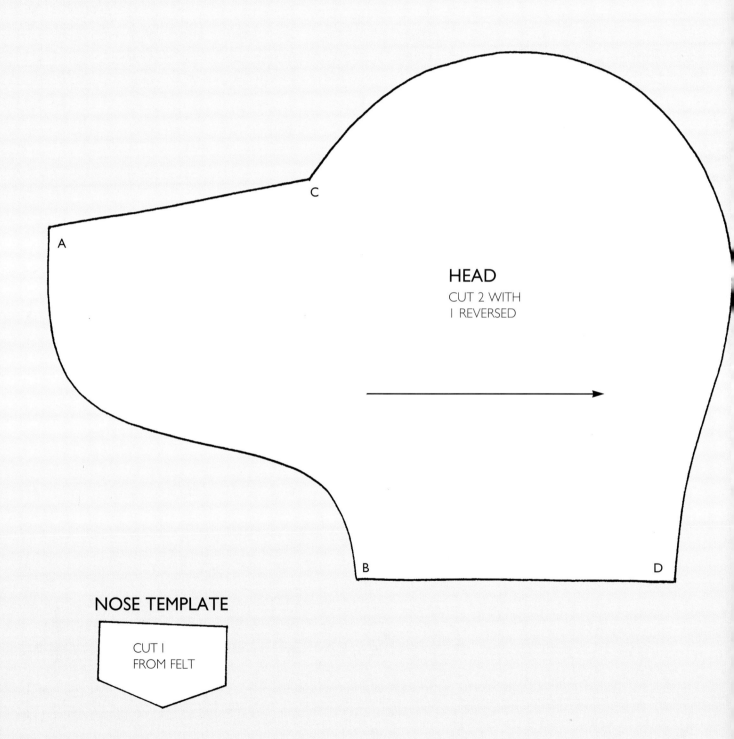

C

A

HEAD
CUT 2 WITH
1 REVERSED

B

D

NOSE TEMPLATE

CUT 1
FROM FELT

ANASTASIA

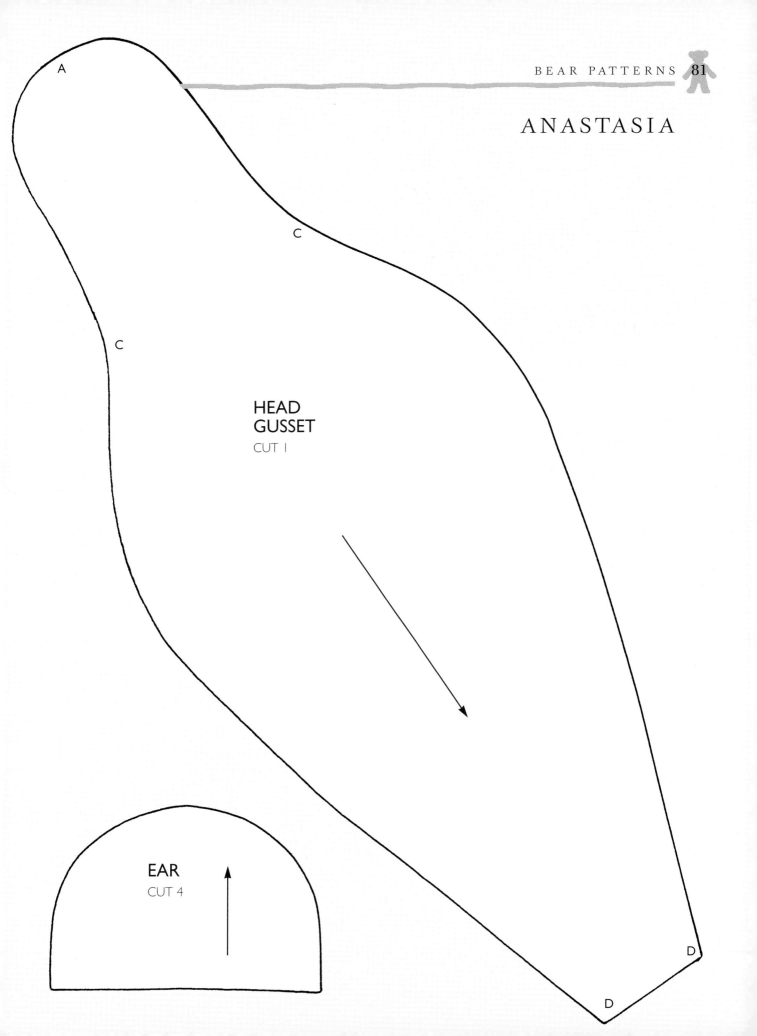

A

C

C

HEAD
GUSSET
CUT I

EAR
CUT 4

D

D

ANASTASIA

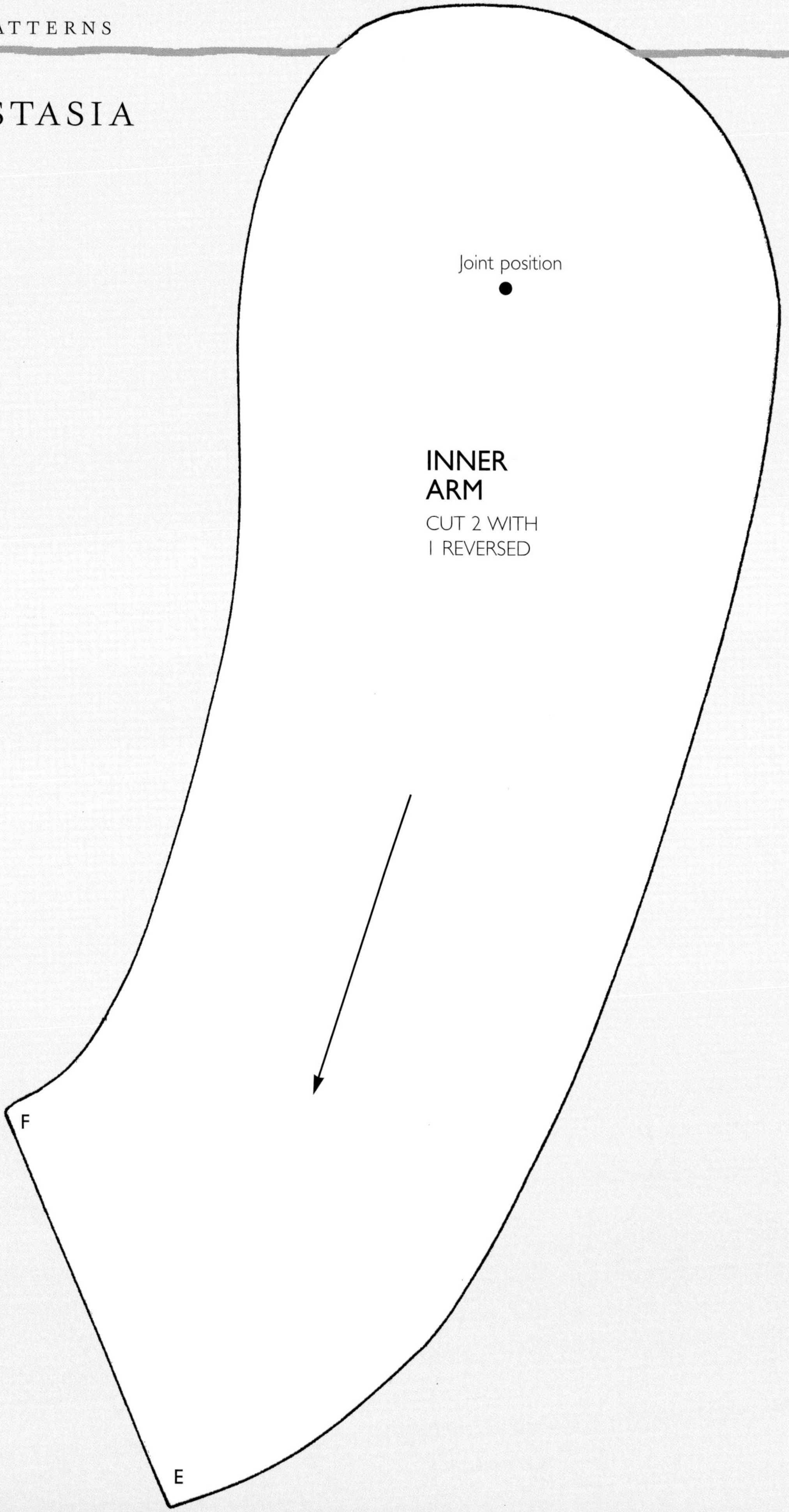

Joint position

**INNER
ARM**

CUT 2 WITH
1 REVERSED

F

E

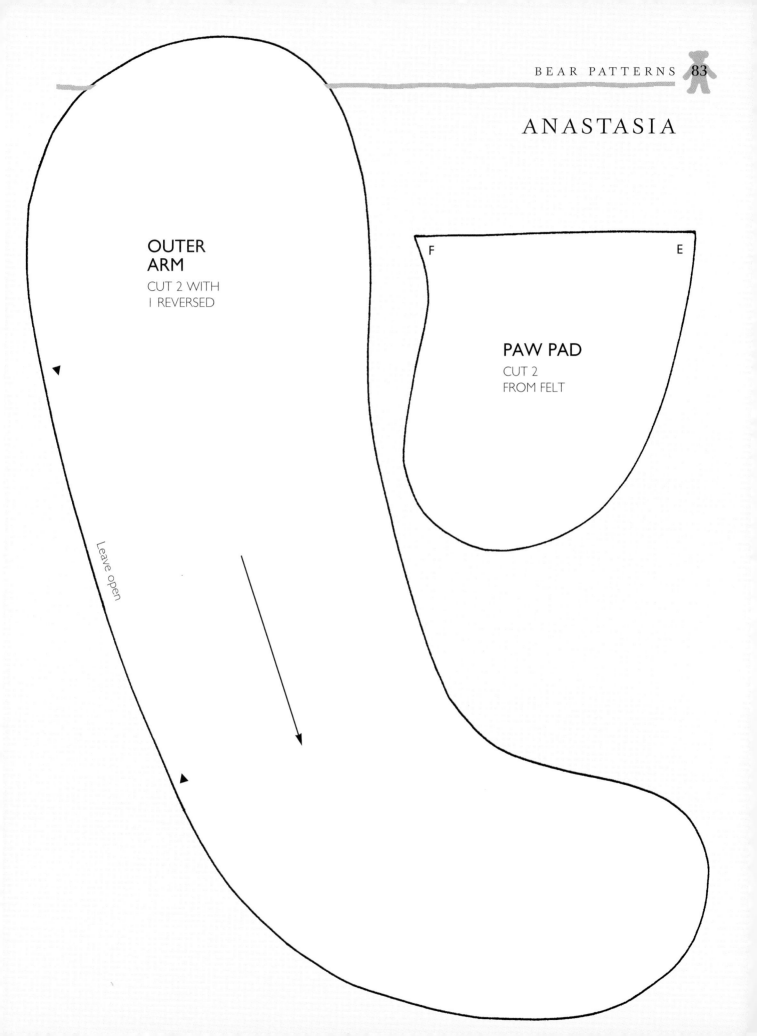

ANASTASIA

OUTER
ARM

CUT 2 WITH
1 REVERSED

Leave open

PAW PAD

CUT 2
FROM FELT

F E

ANASTASIA

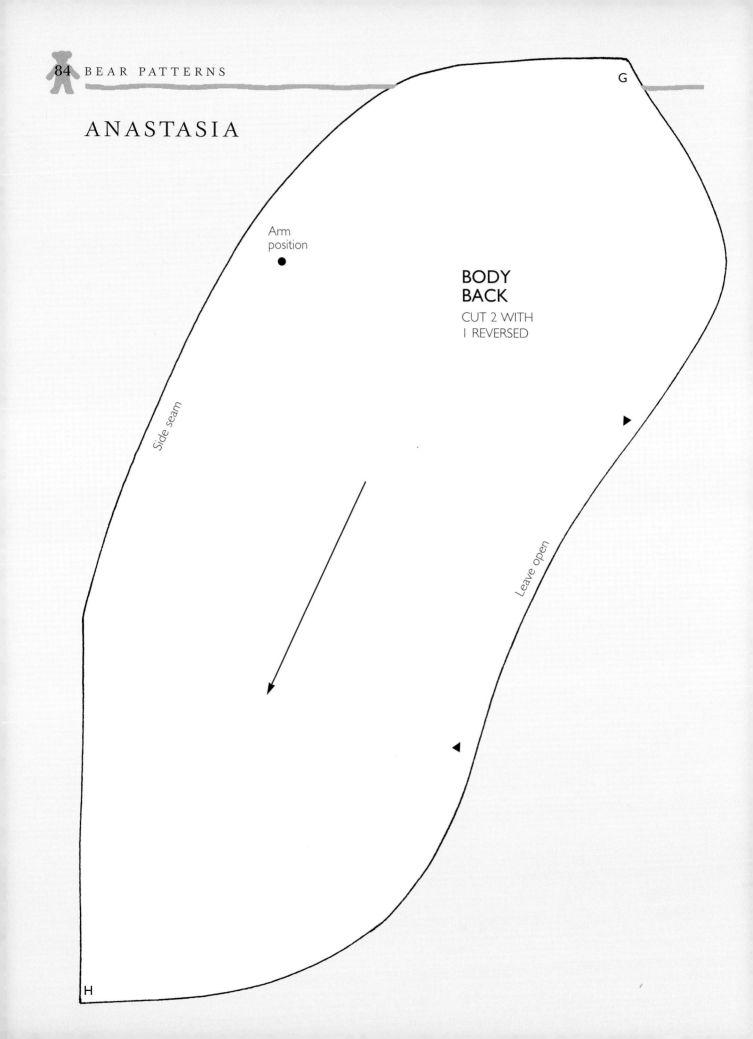

Arm
position

BODY
BACK

CUT 2 WITH
1 REVERSED

Side seam

Leave open

H

G

ANASTASIA

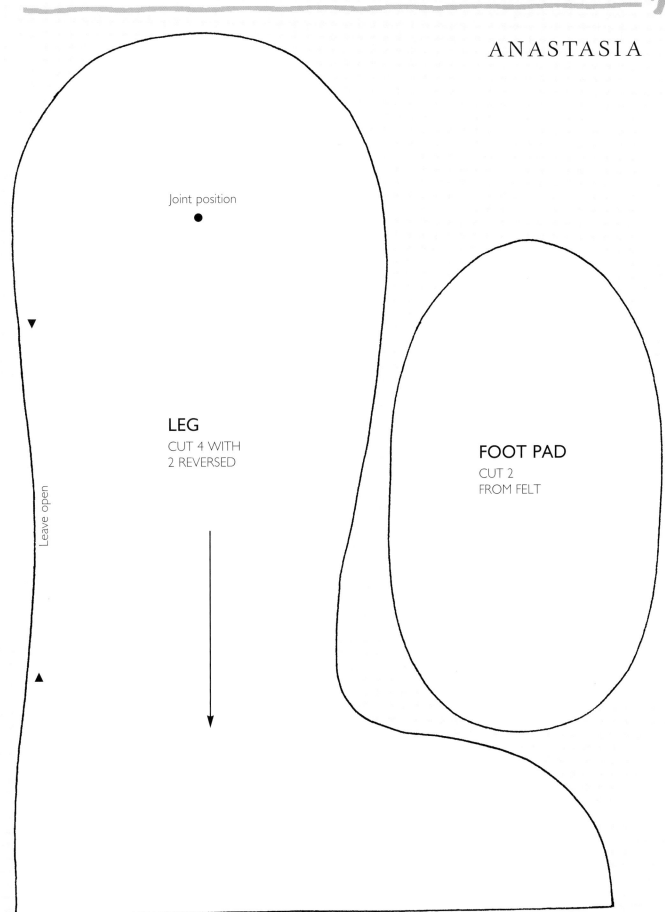

Joint position

Leave open

LEG
CUT 4 WITH
2 REVERSED

FOOT PAD
CUT 2
FROM FELT

ANASTASIA

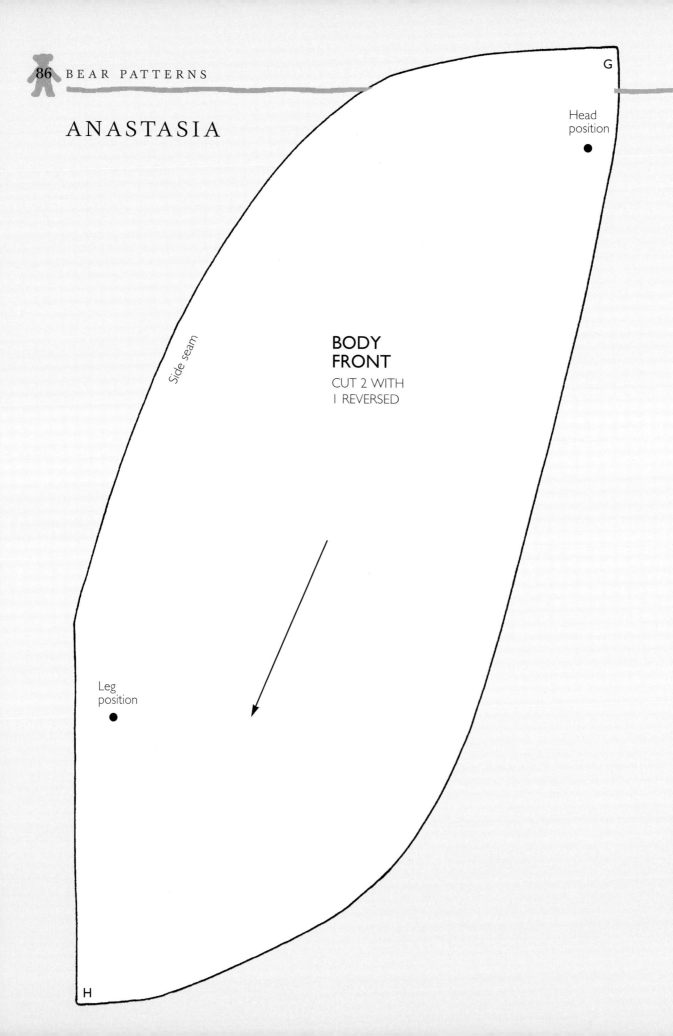

G

Head
position

BODY
FRONT

CUT 2 WITH
1 REVERSED

Side seam

Leg
position

H

DRESS PATTERNS

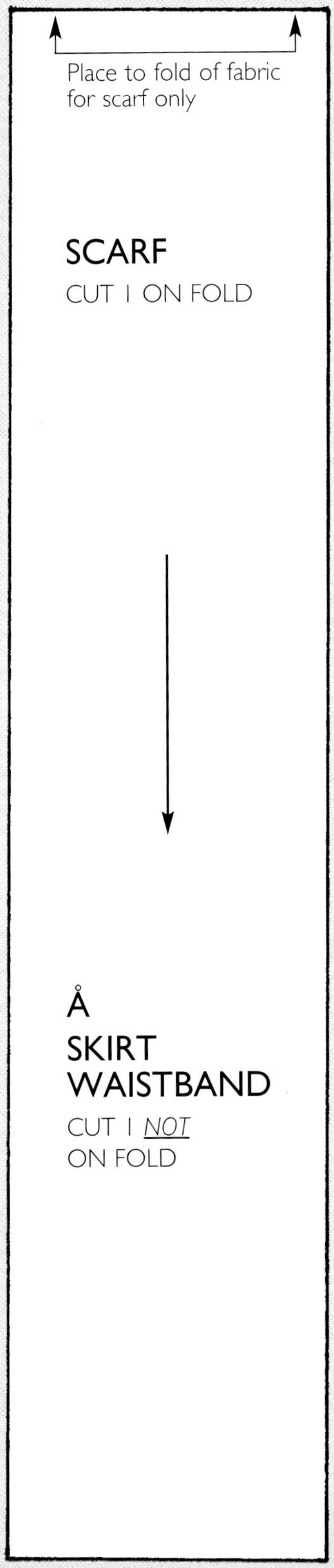

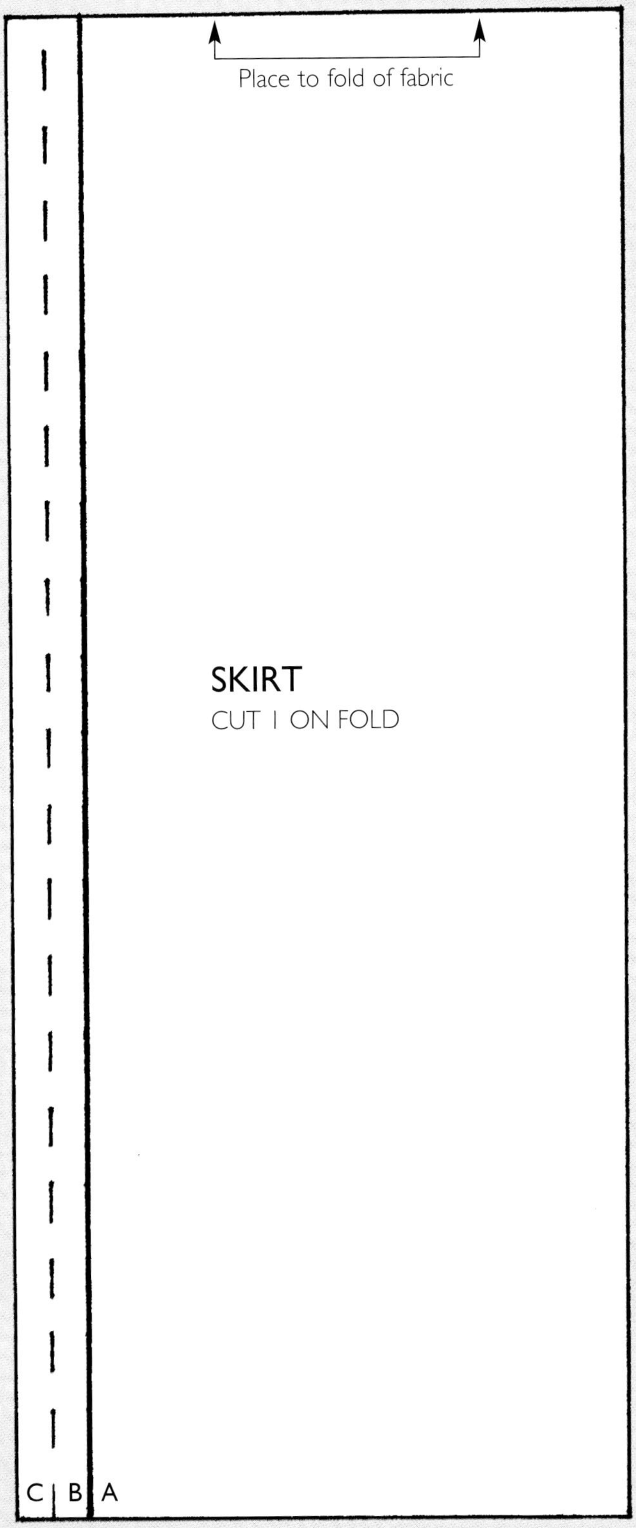

Place to fold of fabric
for scarf only

SCARF

CUT I ON FOLD

Place to fold of fabric

SKIRT

CUT I ON FOLD

Å
**SKIRT
WAISTBAND**

CUT I *NOT*
ON FOLD

C | B | A

GEORGIE'S CLOTHES

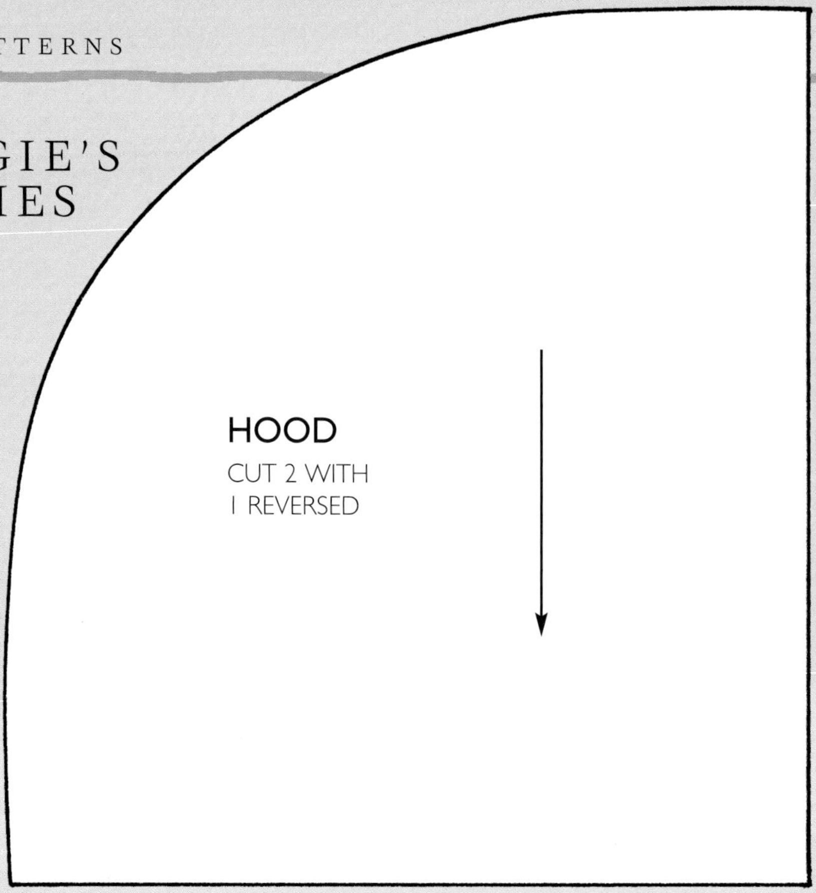

HOOD
CUT 2 WITH
1 REVERSED

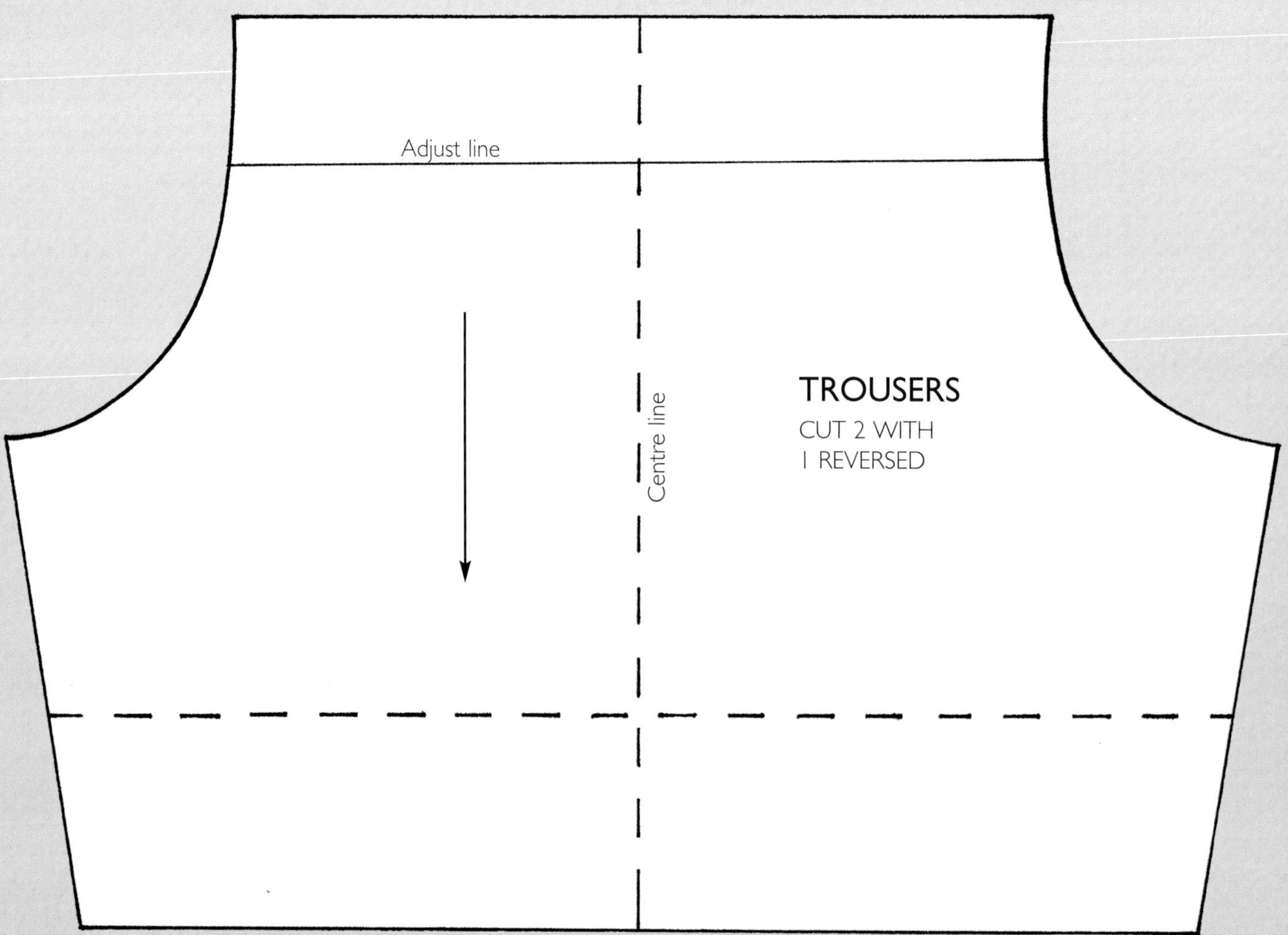

Adjust line

Centre line

TROUSERS
CUT 2 WITH
1 REVERSED

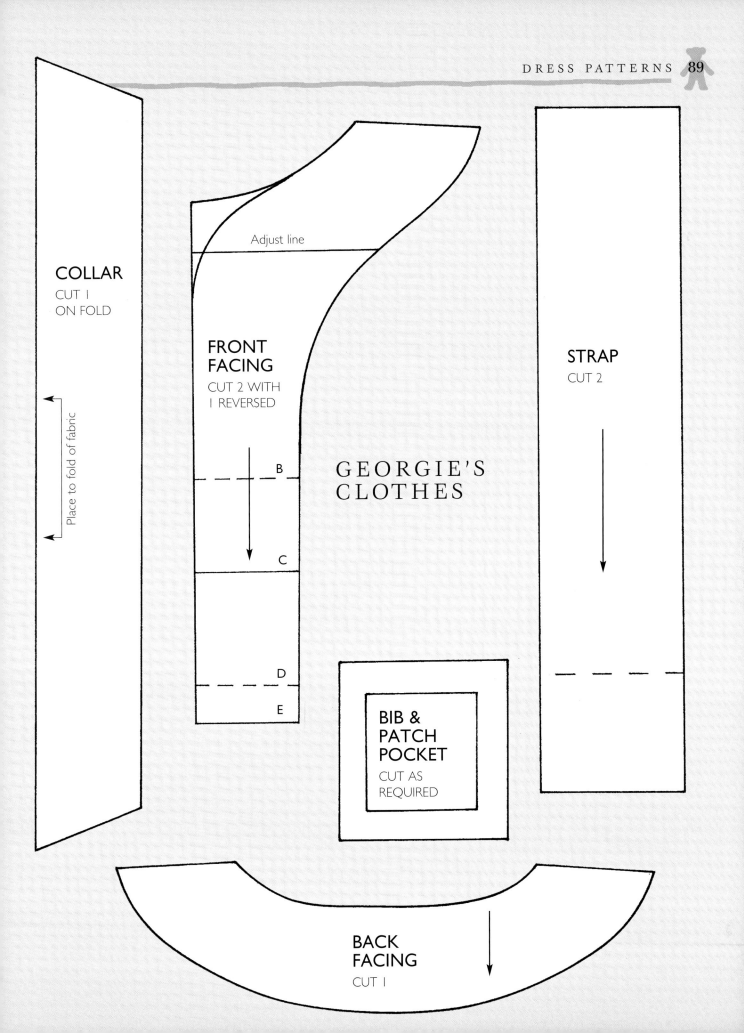

COLLAR

CUT 1
ON FOLD

Place to fold of fabric

Adjust line

**FRONT
FACING**

CUT 2 WITH
1 REVERSED

B

C

D

E

**GEORGIE'S
CLOTHES**

STRAP

CUT 2

**BIB &
PATCH
POCKET**

CUT AS
REQUIRED

**BACK
FACING**

CUT 1

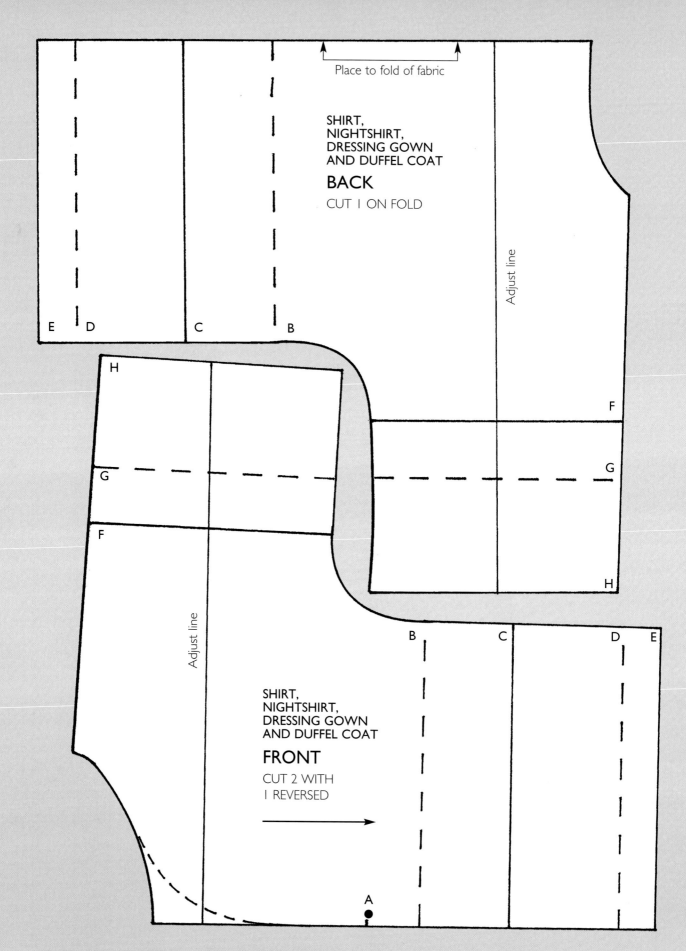

Place to fold of fabric

SHIRT,
NIGHTSHIRT,
DRESSING GOWN
AND DUFFEL COAT
BACK

CUT 1 ON FOLD

Adjust line

E D C B

F

G G

H

F

G

H

Adjust line

SHIRT,
NIGHTSHIRT,
DRESSING GOWN
AND DUFFEL COAT

FRONT

CUT 2 WITH
1 REVERSED

B C D E

A

GEORGIE'S CLOTHES

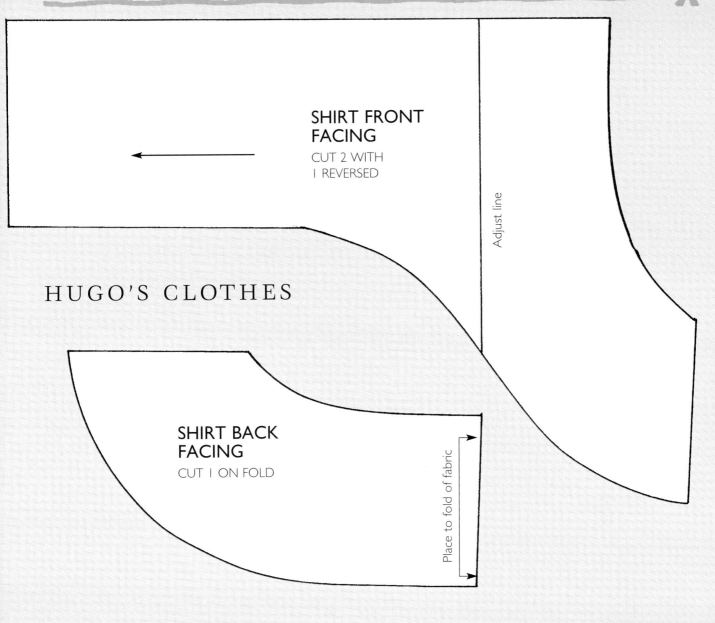

HUGO'S CLOTHES

SHIRT FRONT FACING

CUT 2 WITH
1 REVERSED

Adjust line

SHIRT BACK FACING

CUT 1 ON FOLD

Place to fold of fabric

LEDERHOSEN STRAPS

CUT 2 ON FOLD

Place to fold of fabric

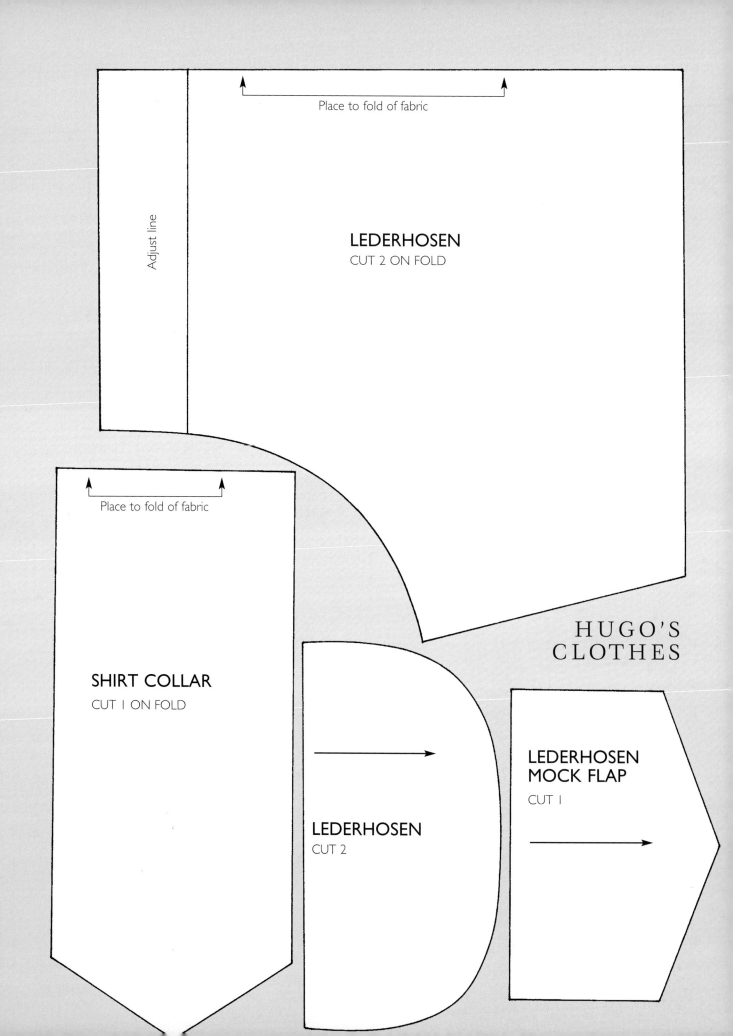

Place to fold of fabric

Adjust line

LEDERHOSEN
CUT 2 ON FOLD

Place to fold of fabric

SHIRT COLLAR
CUT 1 ON FOLD

HUGO'S
CLOTHES

LEDERHOSEN
CUT 2

**LEDERHOSEN
MOCK FLAP**
CUT 1

HUGO'S CLOTHES

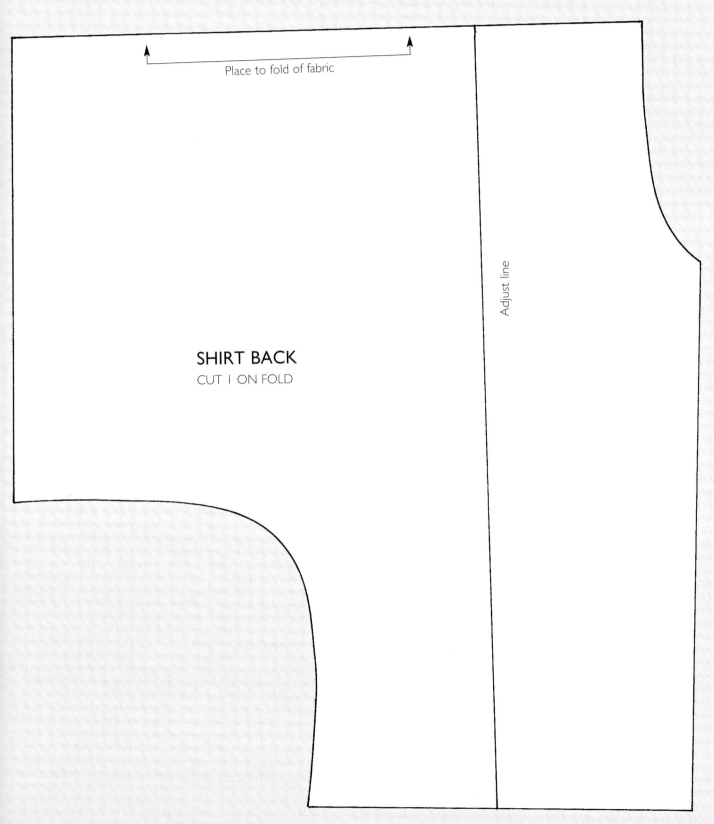

Place to fold of fabric

Adjust line

SHIRT BACK

CUT 1 ON FOLD

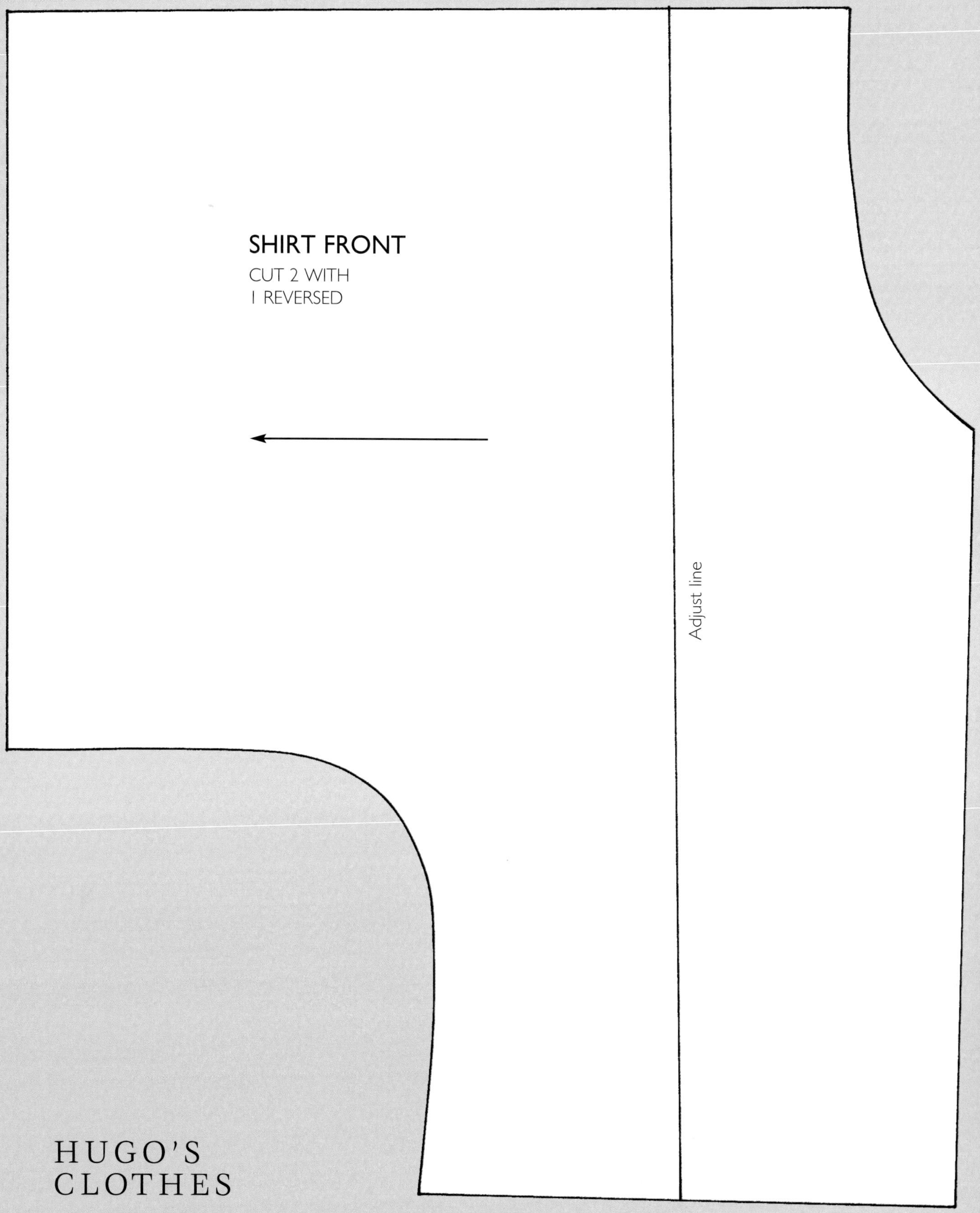
SHIRT FRONT
CUT 2 WITH
1 REVERSED
Adjust line

HUGO'S
CLOTHES

HUGO'S
CLOTHES

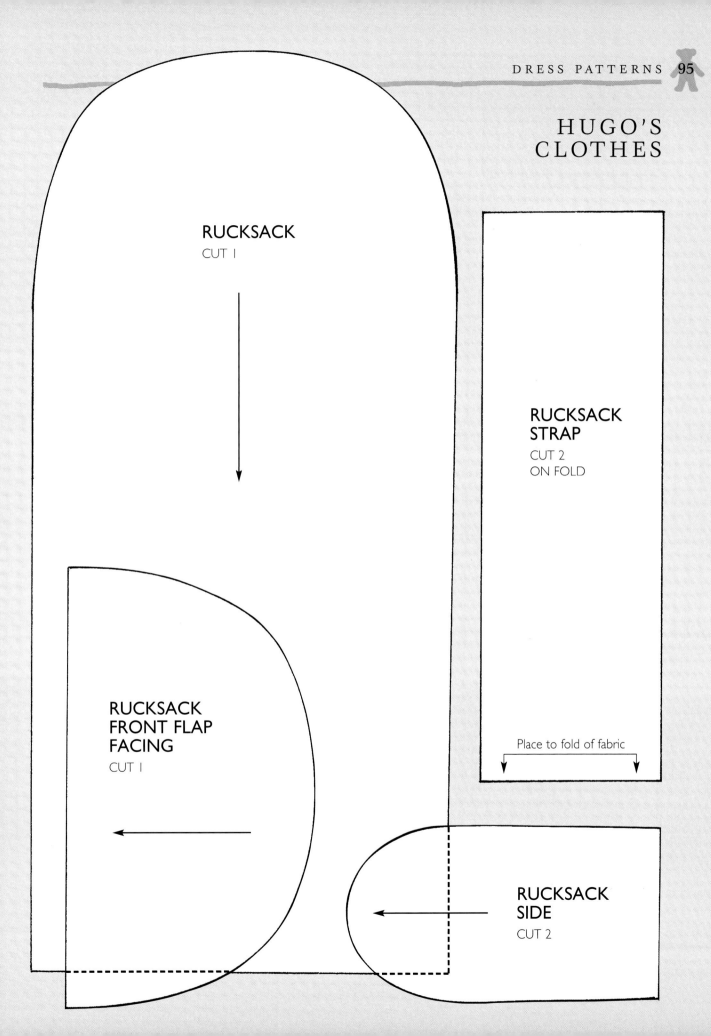

RUCKSACK
CUT 1

RUCKSACK
STRAP
CUT 2
ON FOLD

Place to fold of fabric

RUCKSACK
FRONT FLAP
FACING
CUT 1

RUCKSACK
SIDE
CUT 2

POPPY'S
CLOTHES

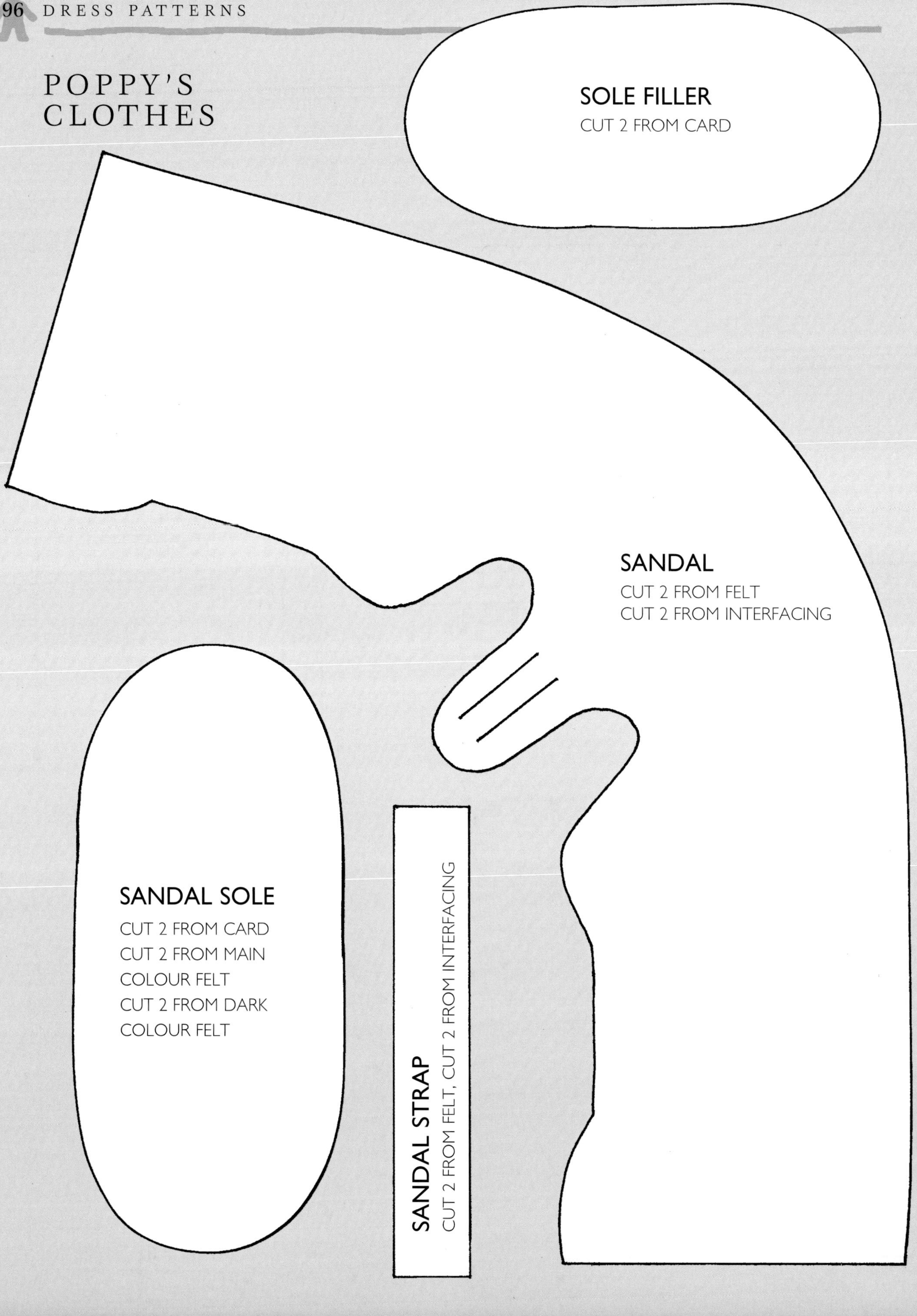

SOLE FILLER

CUT 2 FROM CARD

SANDAL

CUT 2 FROM FELT
CUT 2 FROM INTERFACING

SANDAL SOLE

CUT 2 FROM CARD
CUT 2 FROM MAIN
COLOUR FELT
CUT 2 FROM DARK
COLOUR FELT

SANDAL STRAP

CUT 2 FROM FELT, CUT 2 FROM INTERFACING

POPPY'S
CLOTHES

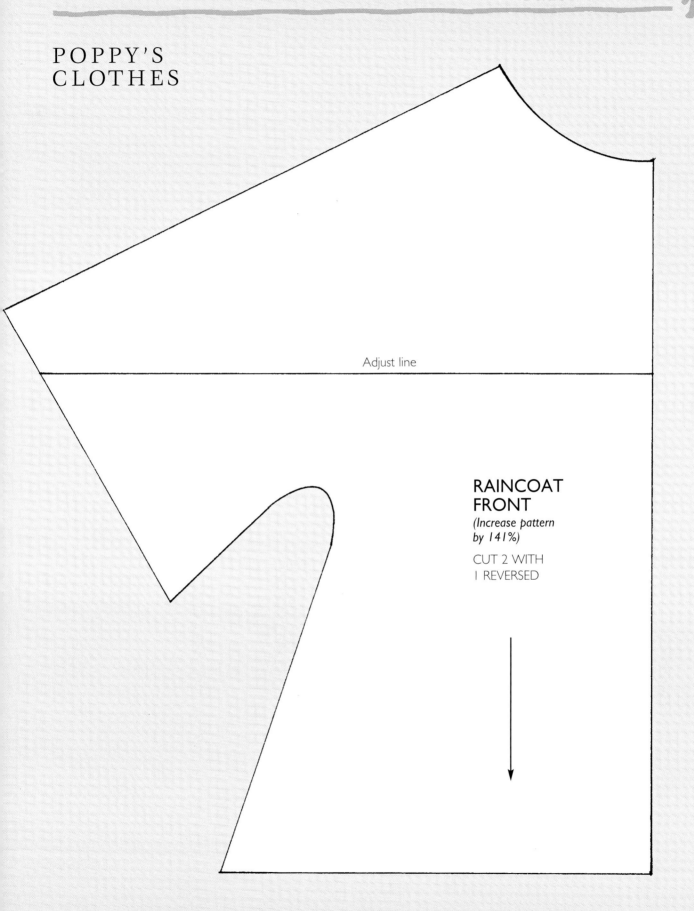

Adjust line

RAINCOAT
FRONT
*(Increase pattern
by 141%)*

CUT 2 WITH
1 REVERSED

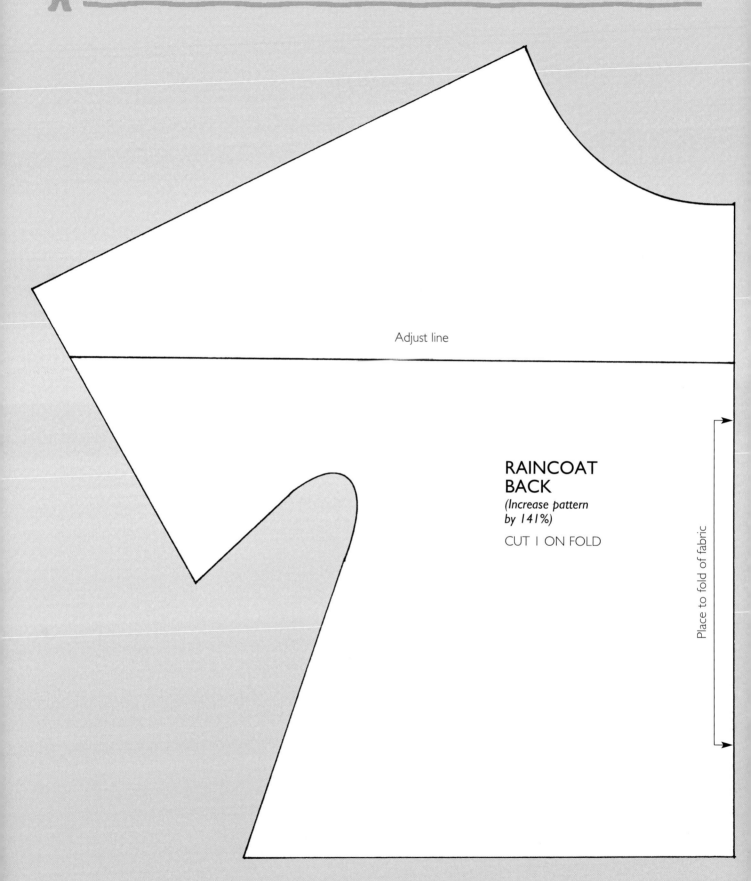

Adjust line

**RAINCOAT
BACK**
*(Increase pattern
by 141%)*

CUT 1 ON FOLD

Place to fold of fabric

POPPY'S CLOTHES

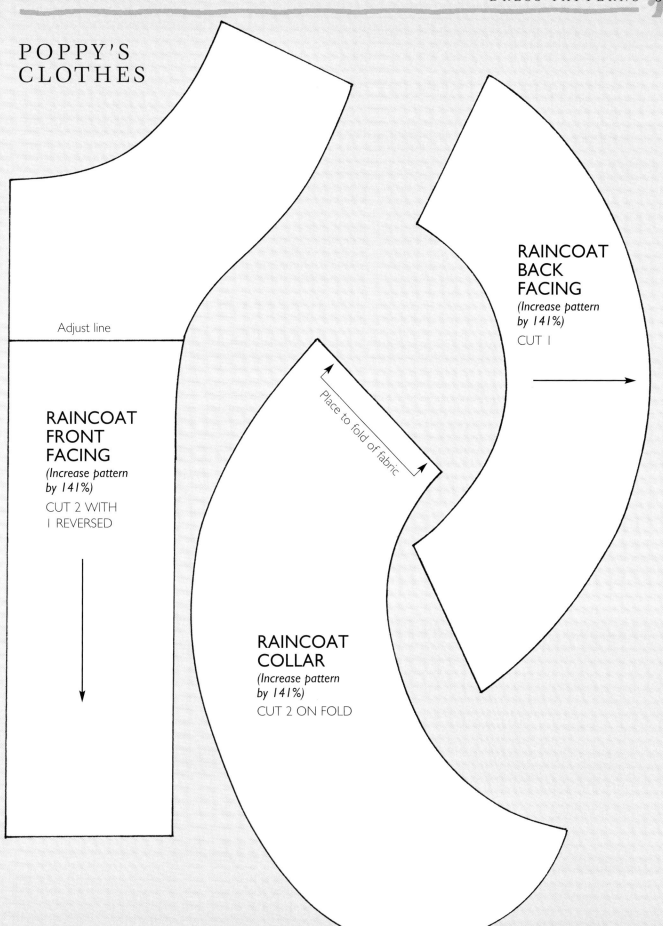

Adjust line

RAINCOAT FRONT FACING
(Increase pattern by 141%)
CUT 2 WITH 1 REVERSED

Place to fold of fabric

RAINCOAT BACK FACING
(Increase pattern by 141%)
CUT 1

RAINCOAT COLLAR
(Increase pattern by 141%)
CUT 2 ON FOLD

POPPY'S
CLOTHES

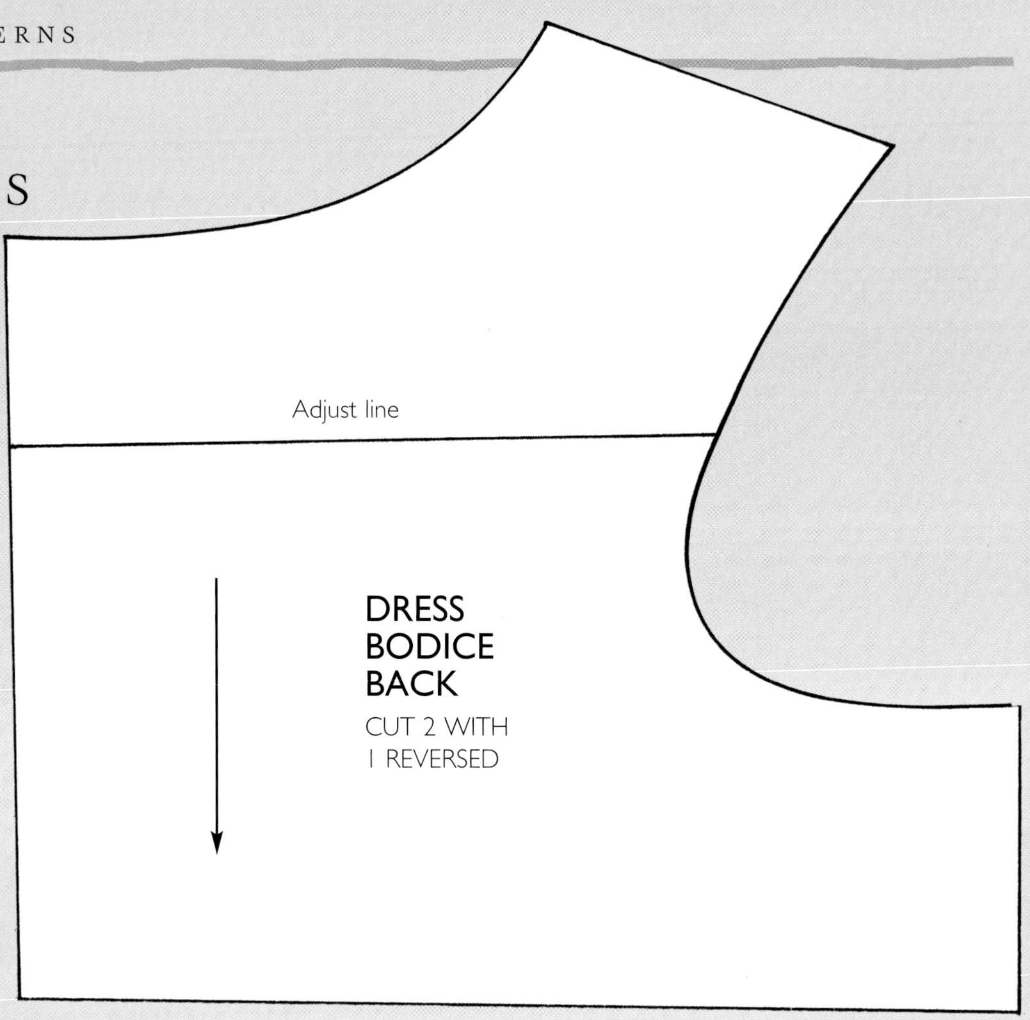

Adjust line

DRESS
BODICE
BACK

CUT 2 WITH
1 REVERSED

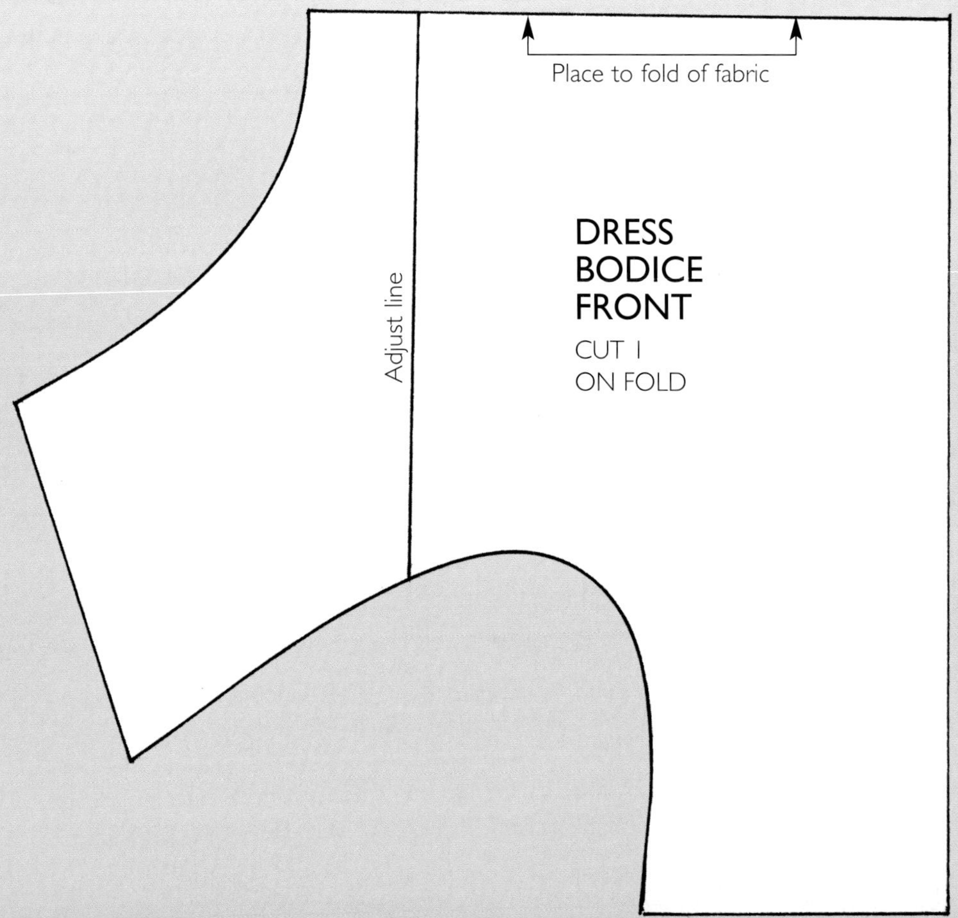

Place to fold of fabric

Adjust line

DRESS
BODICE
FRONT

CUT 1
ON FOLD

POPPY'S
CLOTHES

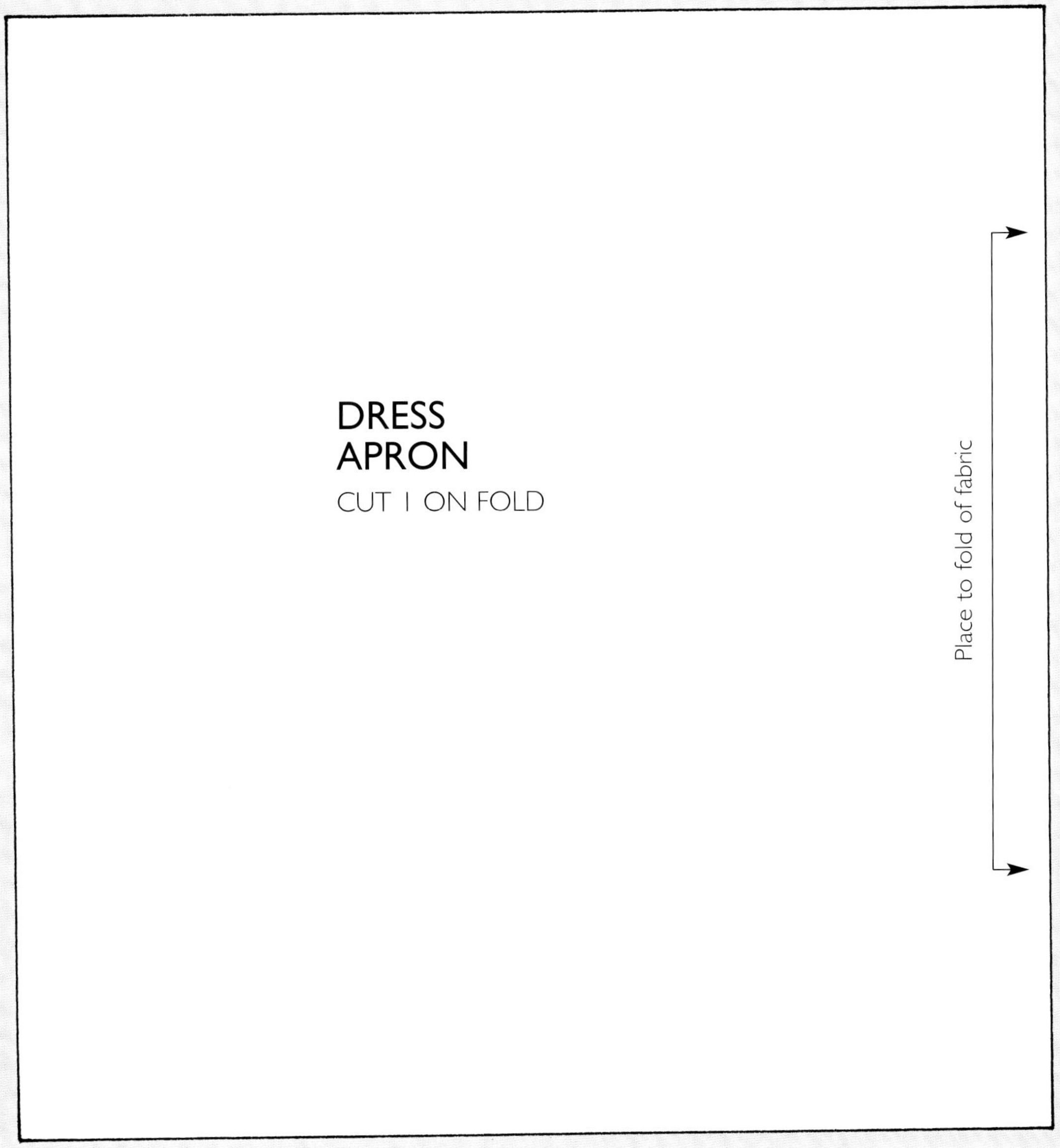

DRESS
APRON
CUT 1 ON FOLD

Place to fold of fabric

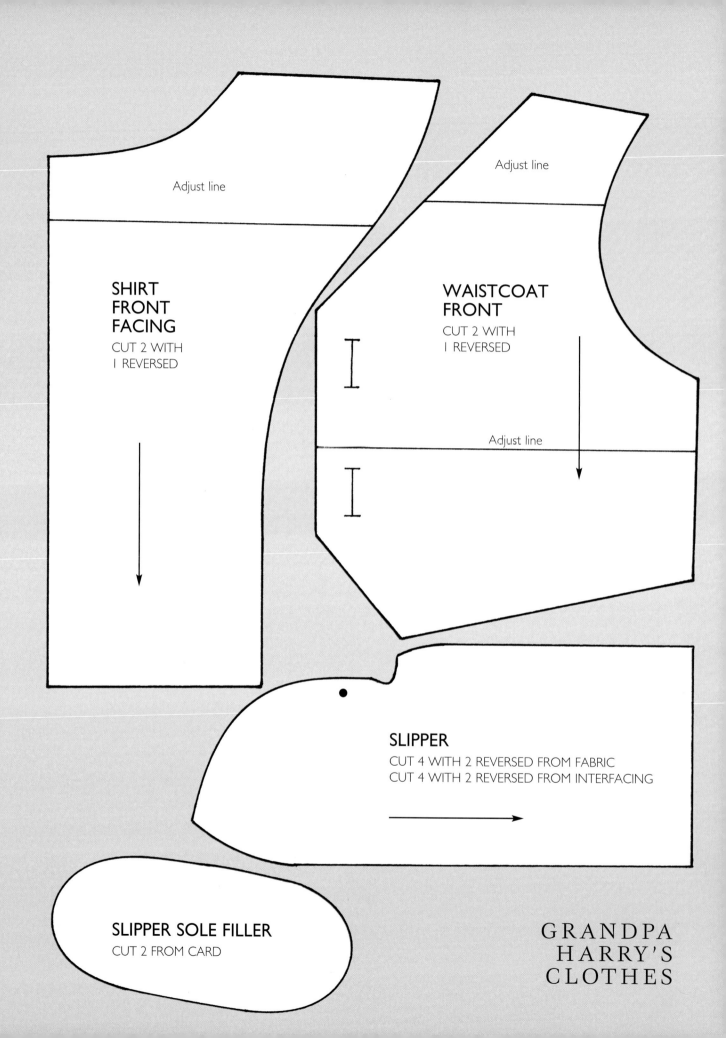

SHIRT
FRONT
FACING

CUT 2 WITH
1 REVERSED

Adjust line

WAISTCOAT
FRONT

CUT 2 WITH
1 REVERSED

Adjust line

Adjust line

SLIPPER

CUT 4 WITH 2 REVERSED FROM FABRIC
CUT 4 WITH 2 REVERSED FROM INTERFACING

SLIPPER SOLE FILLER

CUT 2 FROM CARD

GRANDPA
HARRY'S
CLOTHES

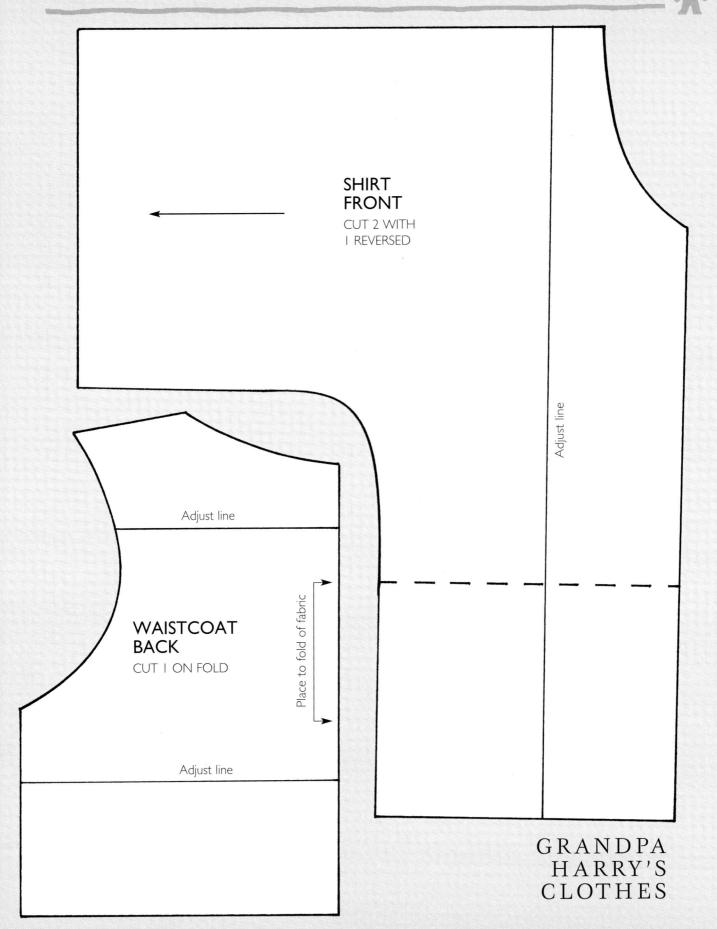

SHIRT
FRONT

CUT 2 WITH
1 REVERSED

Adjust line

Adjust line

WAISTCOAT
BACK

CUT 1 ON FOLD

Place to fold of fabric

Adjust line

GRANDPA
HARRY'S
CLOTHES

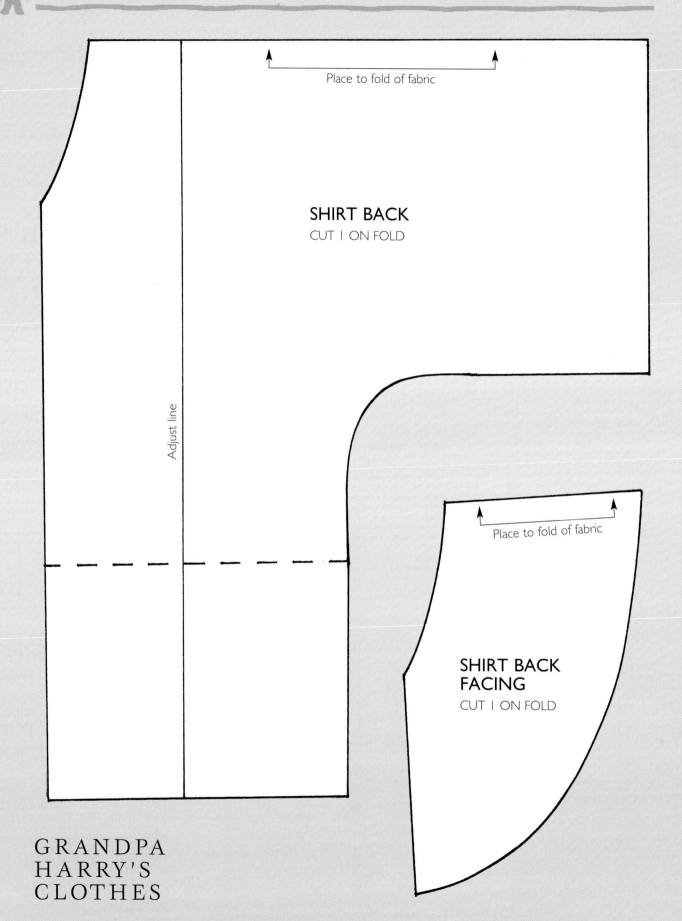

Place to fold of fabric

SHIRT BACK
CUT 1 ON FOLD

Adjust line

Place to fold of fabric

SHIRT BACK FACING
CUT 1 ON FOLD

GRANDPA
HARRY'S
CLOTHES

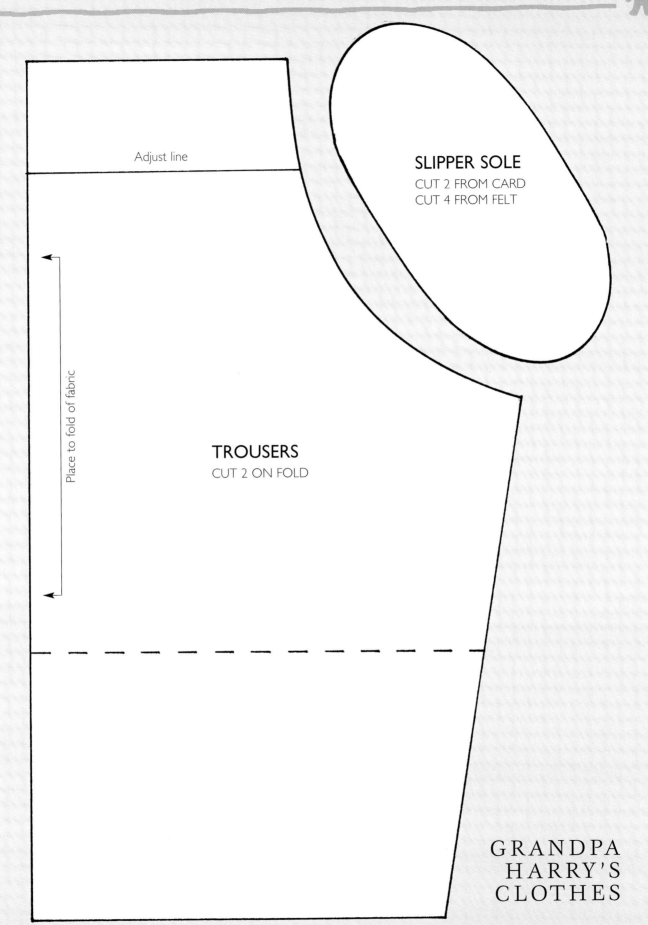

Adjust line

Place to fold of fabric

SLIPPER SOLE
CUT 2 FROM CARD
CUT 4 FROM FELT

TROUSERS
CUT 2 ON FOLD

GRANDPA
HARRY'S
CLOTHES

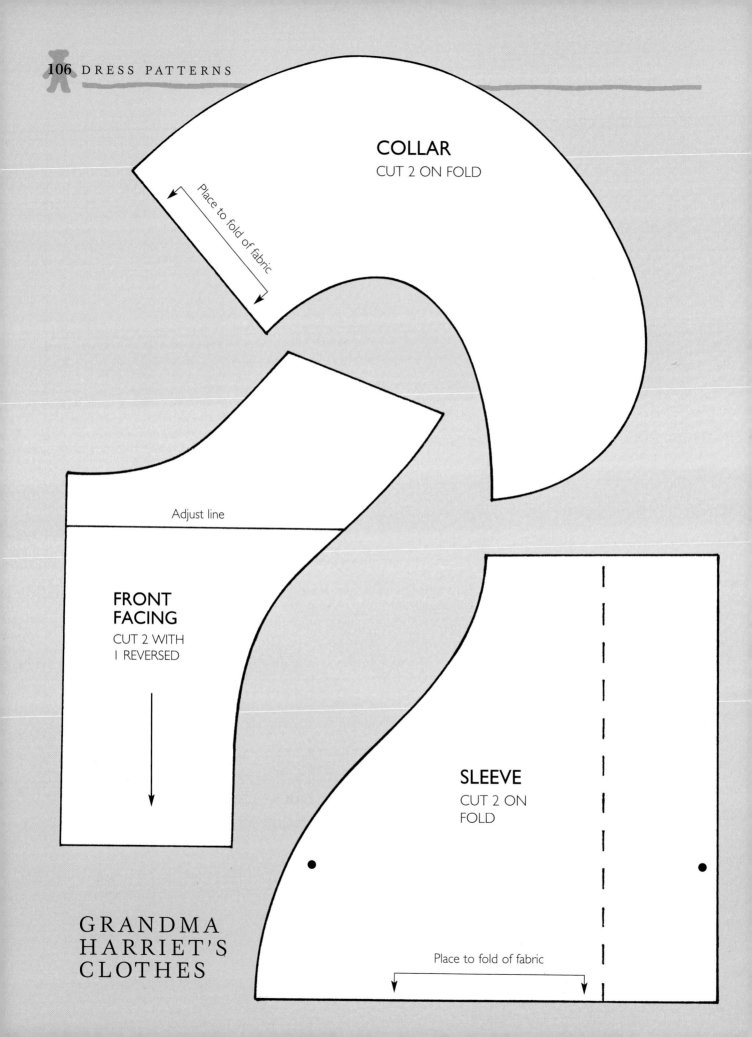

COLLAR
CUT 2 ON FOLD

Place to fold of fabric

Adjust line

FRONT
FACING
CUT 2 WITH
1 REVERSED

SLEEVE
CUT 2 ON
FOLD

GRANDMA
HARRIET'S
CLOTHES

Place to fold of fabric

GRANDMA HARRIET'S CLOTHES

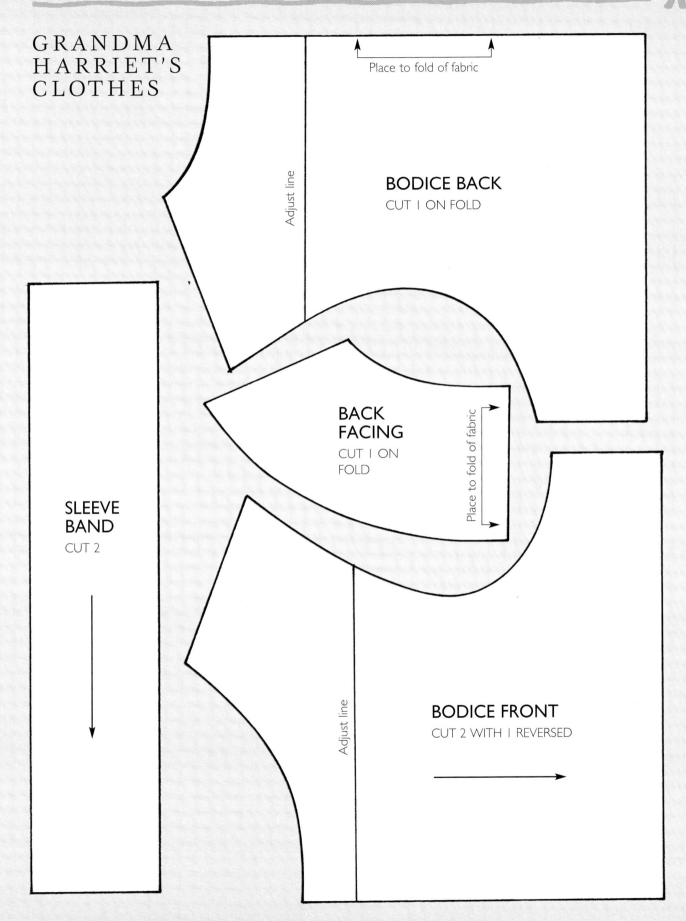

Place to fold of fabric

Adjust line

BODICE BACK

CUT 1 ON FOLD

BACK FACING

CUT 1 ON FOLD

Place to fold of fabric

SLEEVE BAND

CUT 2

Adjust line

BODICE FRONT

CUT 2 WITH 1 REVERSED

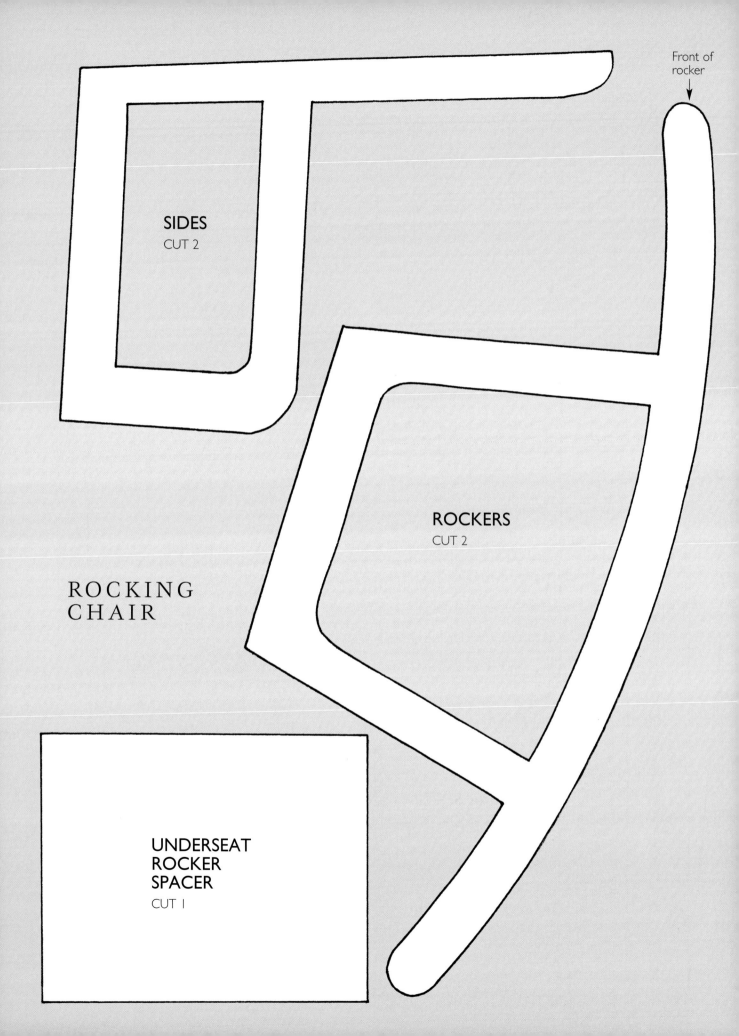

Front of
rocker

SIDES
CUT 2

ROCKERS
CUT 2

ROCKING
CHAIR

UNDERSEAT
ROCKER
SPACER

CUT 1

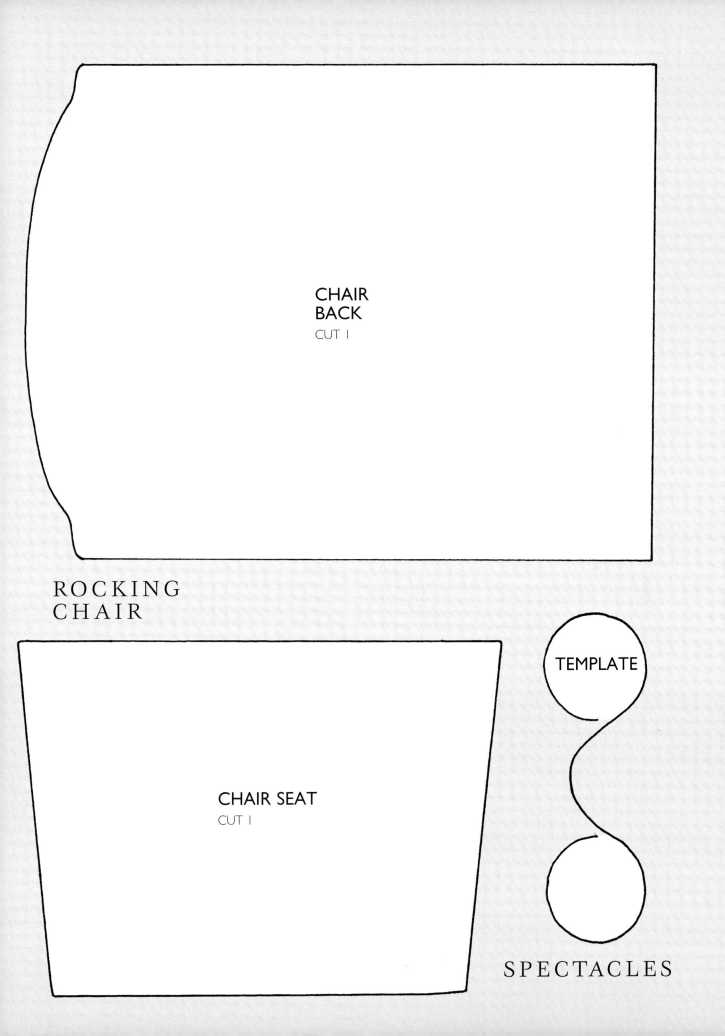

CHAIR
BACK
CUT 1

ROCKING
CHAIR

CHAIR SEAT
CUT 1

TEMPLATE

SPECTACLES

MEI YING'S
CLOTHES

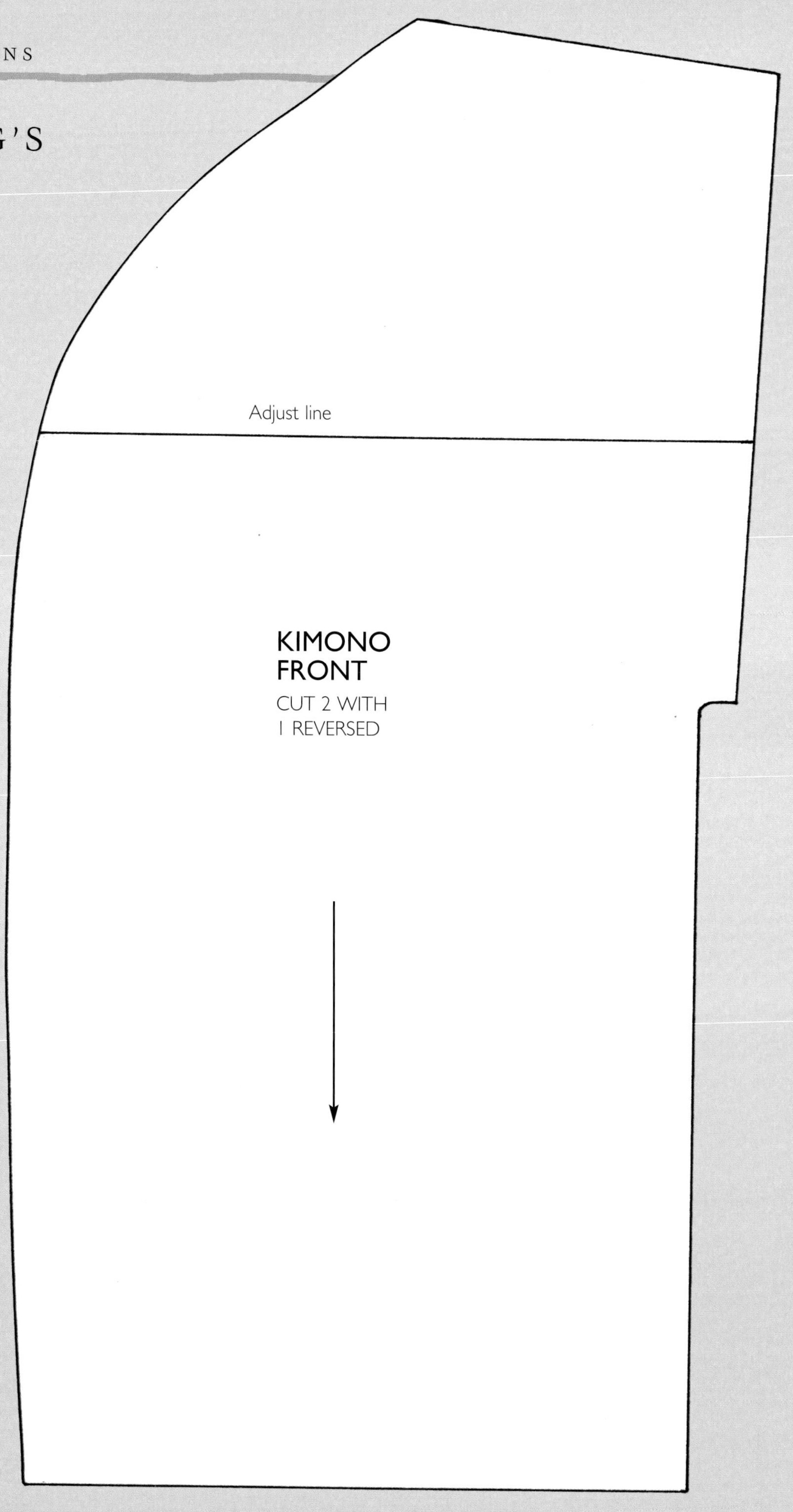

Adjust line

**KIMONO
FRONT**

CUT 2 WITH
1 REVERSED

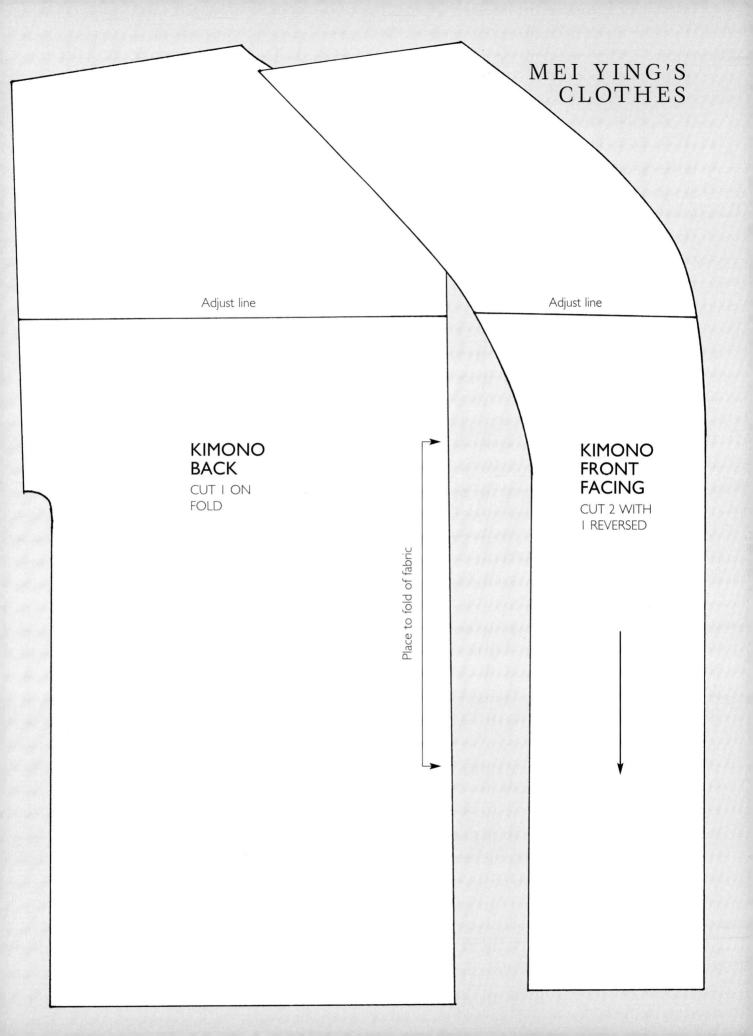

MEI YING'S
CLOTHES

Adjust line

Adjust line

**KIMONO
BACK**

CUT 1 ON
FOLD

Place to fold of fabric

**KIMONO
FRONT
FACING**

CUT 2 WITH
1 REVERSED

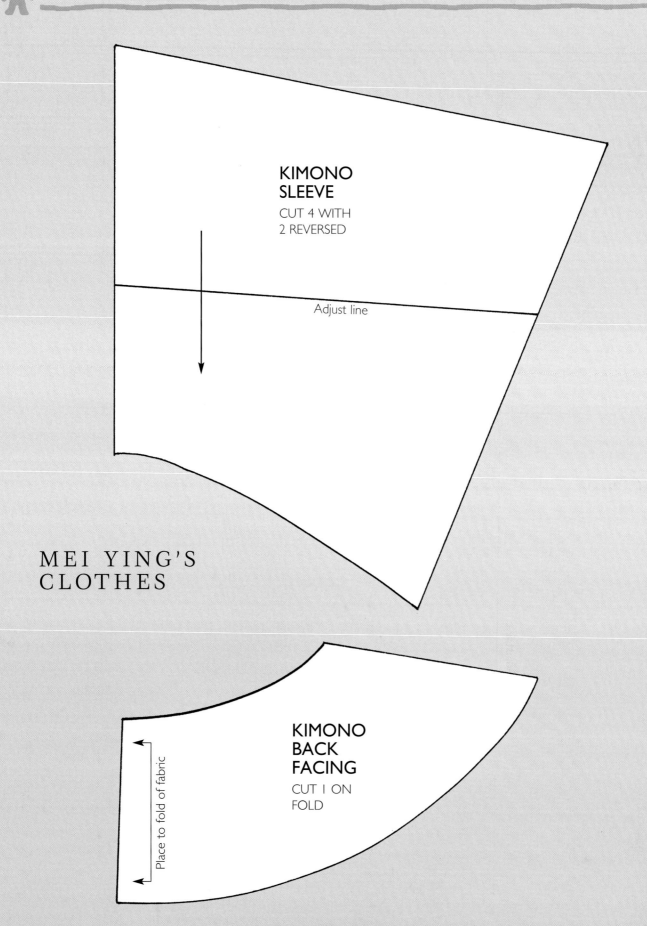

KIMONO
SLEEVE

CUT 4 WITH
2 REVERSED

Adjust line

MEI YING'S
CLOTHES

KIMONO
BACK
FACING

CUT 1 ON
FOLD

Place to fold of fabric

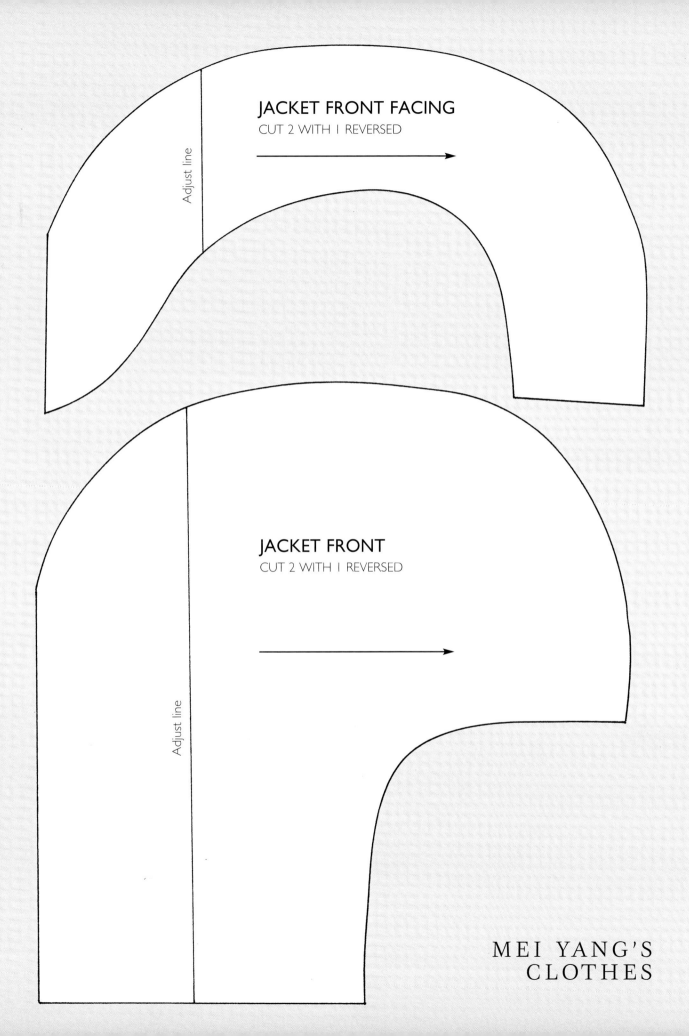

JACKET FRONT FACING
CUT 2 WITH 1 REVERSED

Adjust line

JACKET FRONT
CUT 2 WITH 1 REVERSED

Adjust line

MEI YANG'S
CLOTHES

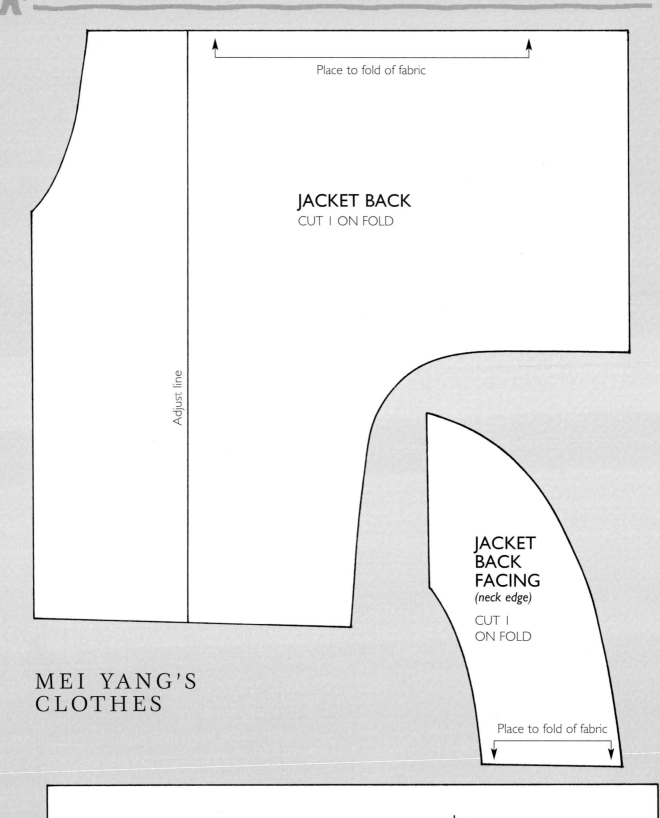

Place to fold of fabric

JACKET BACK

CUT 1 ON FOLD

Adjust line

JACKET
BACK
FACING
(neck edge)

CUT 1
ON FOLD

Place to fold of fabric

MEI YANG'S
CLOTHES

JACKET
BACK FACING
(bottom edge)

CUT 1

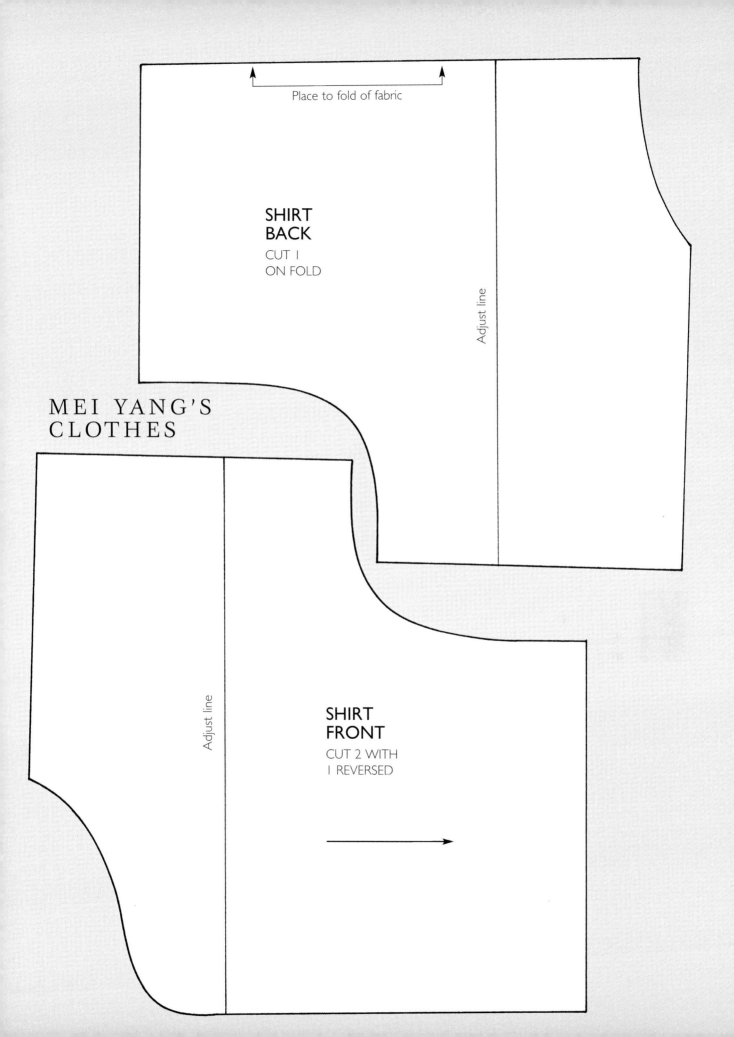

Place to fold of fabric

**SHIRT
BACK**

CUT 1
ON FOLD

Adjust line

MEI YANG'S
CLOTHES

Adjust line

**SHIRT
FRONT**

CUT 2 WITH
1 REVERSED

MEI YANG'S CLOTHES

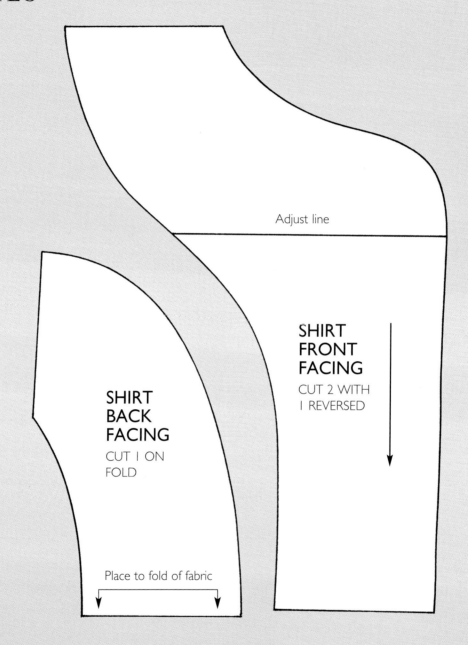

Adjust line

**SHIRT
FRONT
FACING**

CUT 2 WITH
1 REVERSED

**SHIRT
BACK
FACING**

CUT 1 ON
FOLD

Place to fold of fabric

SHIRT COLLAR

CUT 2 ON FOLD

Place to fold of fabric

MEI YANG'S
CLOTHES

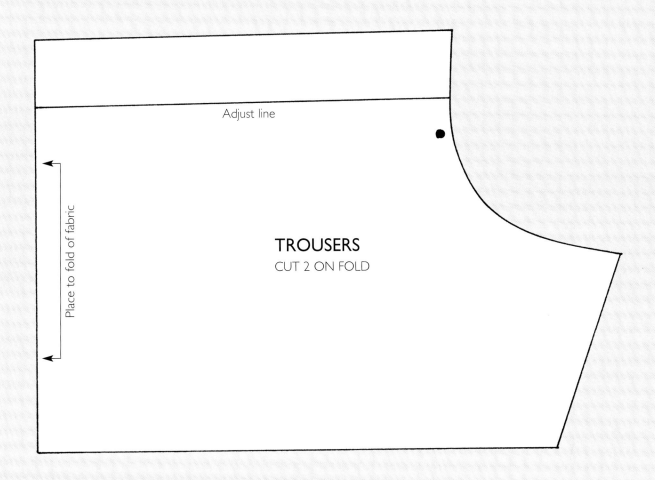

Adjust line

Place to fold of fabric

TROUSERS
CUT 2 ON FOLD

Place to fold of fabric

**TROUSER
WAISTBAND**
CUT 1 ON FOLD

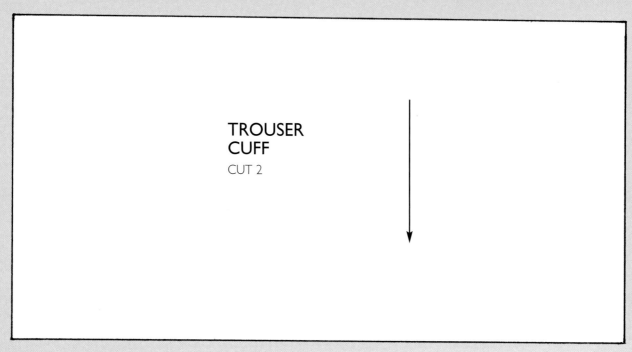

TROUSER
CUFF
CUT 2

MEI YANG'S
CLOTHES

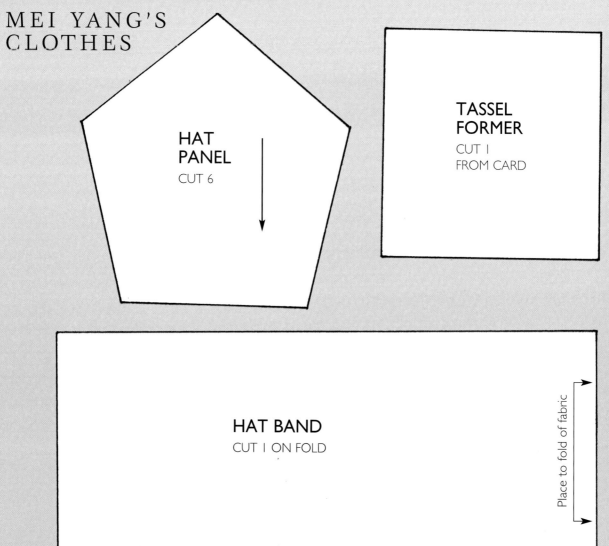

HAT
PANEL
CUT 6

TASSEL
FORMER
CUT 1
FROM CARD

HAT BAND
CUT 1 ON FOLD

Place to fold of fabric

ANASTASIA'S CLOTHES

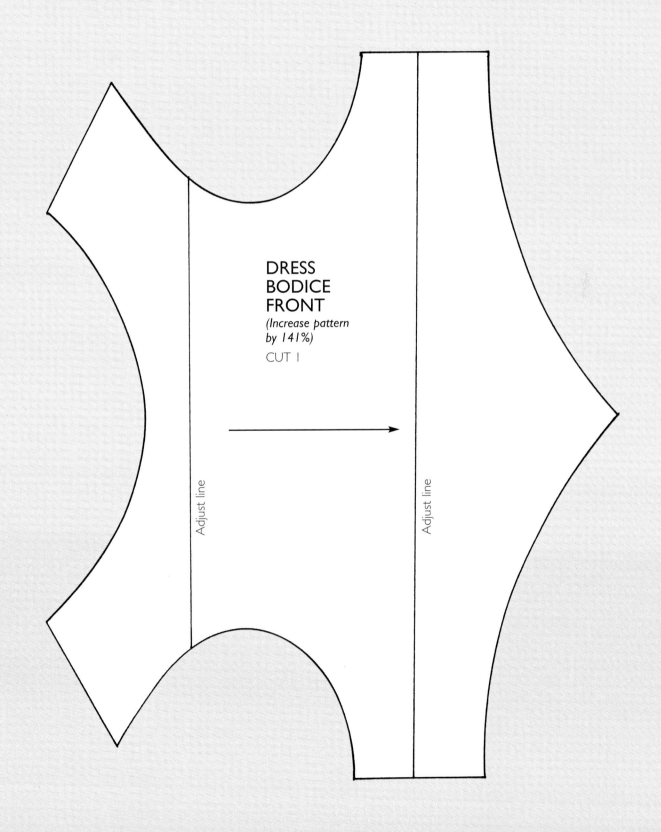

DRESS
BODICE
FRONT
*(Increase pattern
by 141%)*
CUT 1

Adjust line

Adjust line

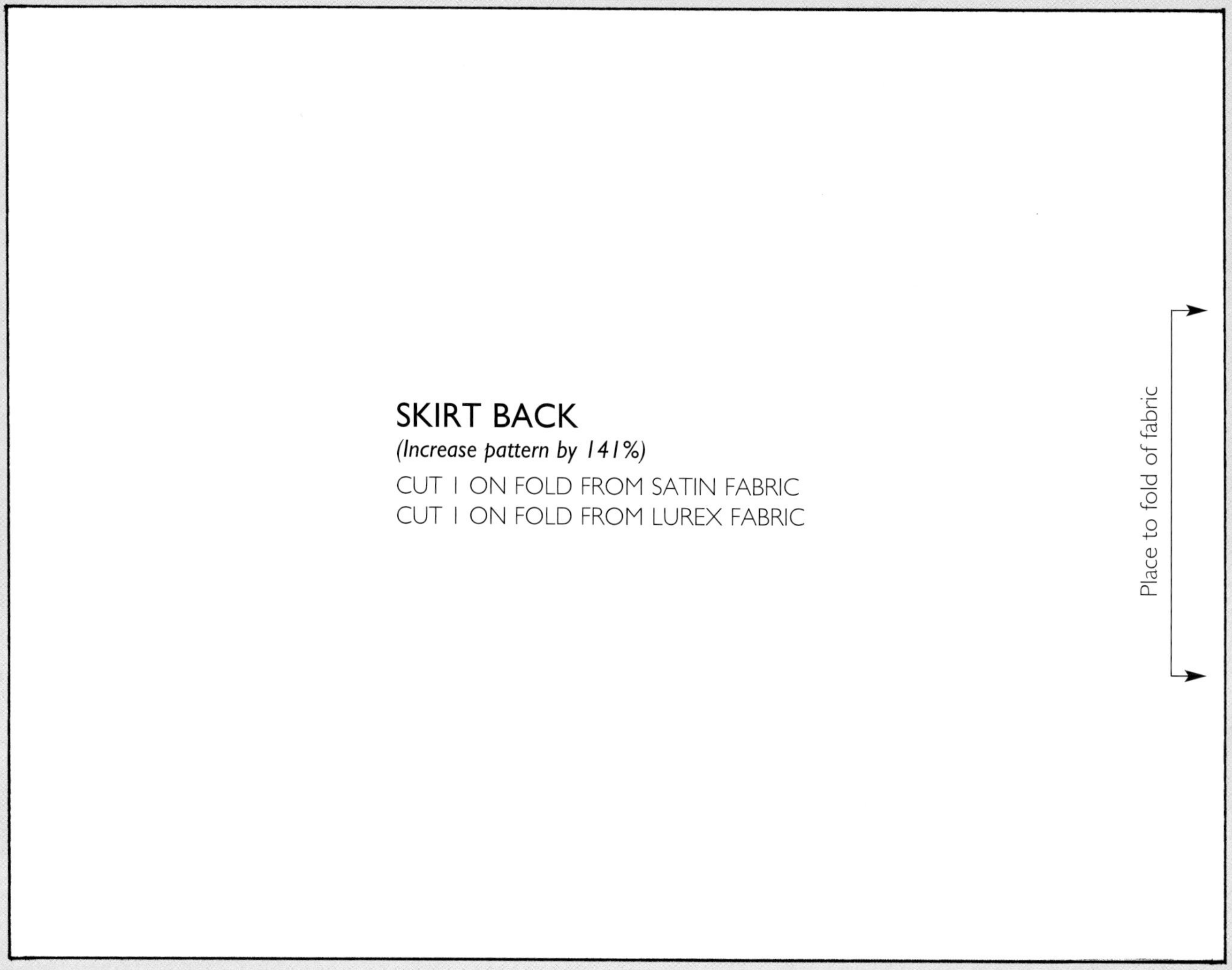

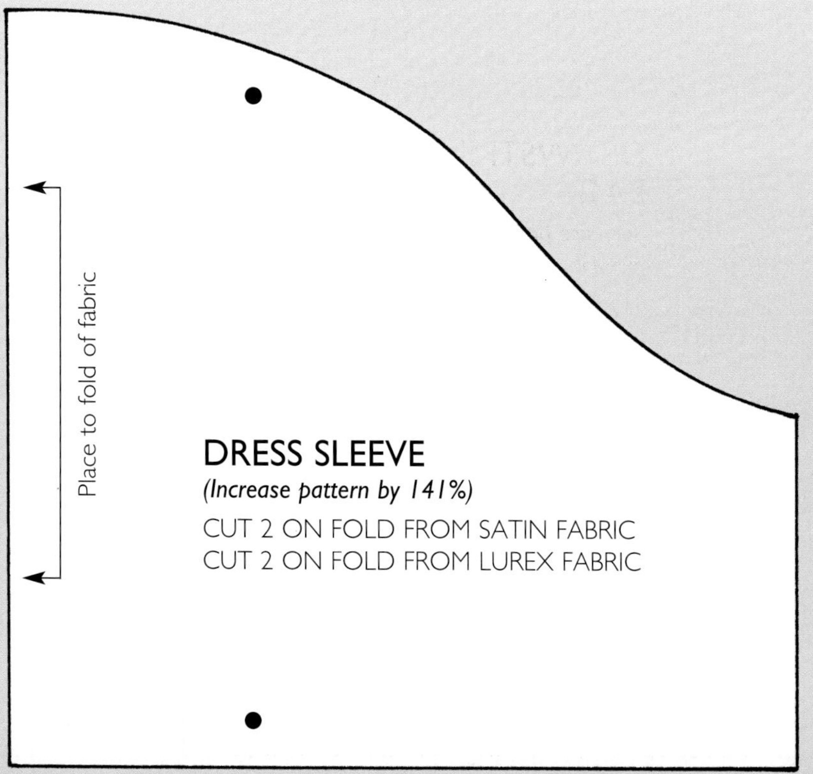

SKIRT BACK
(Increase pattern by 141%)

CUT 1 ON FOLD FROM SATIN FABRIC
CUT 1 ON FOLD FROM LUREX FABRIC

Place to fold of fabric

DRESS SLEEVE
(Increase pattern by 141%)

CUT 2 ON FOLD FROM SATIN FABRIC
CUT 2 ON FOLD FROM LUREX FABRIC

Place to fold of fabric

ANASTASIA'S CLOTHES

Adjust line

BODICE BACK
(Increase pattern by 141%)

CUT 2 WITH
1 REVERSED

SLEEVE BAND
(Increase pattern by 141%)

CUT 2

ANASTASIA'S CLOTHES

Place to fold of fabric

DRAWSTRING BAG
(Increase pattern by 141%)

CUT 1 ON FOLD

DRAWSTRING BAG & FUR HAT TOP
(Increase pattern by 141%)

CUT 1 FOR EACH
AND 1 FROM LINING
FOR HAT

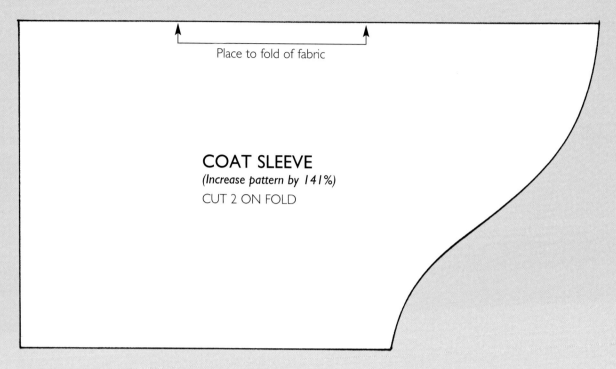

Place to fold of fabric

COAT SLEEVE
(Increase pattern by 141%)
CUT 2 ON FOLD

ANASTASIA'S CLOTHES

Place to fold of fabric

SKIRT FRONT
(Increase pattern by 141%)
CUT 1 ON FOLD FROM SATIN FABRIC
CUT 1 ON FOLD FROM LUREX FABRIC

ANASTASIA'S
CLOTHES

CLOAK HOOD
(Increase pattern by 141%)

CUT 2 WITH 1 REVERSED FROM FABRIC
CUT 2 WITH 1 REVERSED FROM LINING

ANASTASIA'S CLOTHES

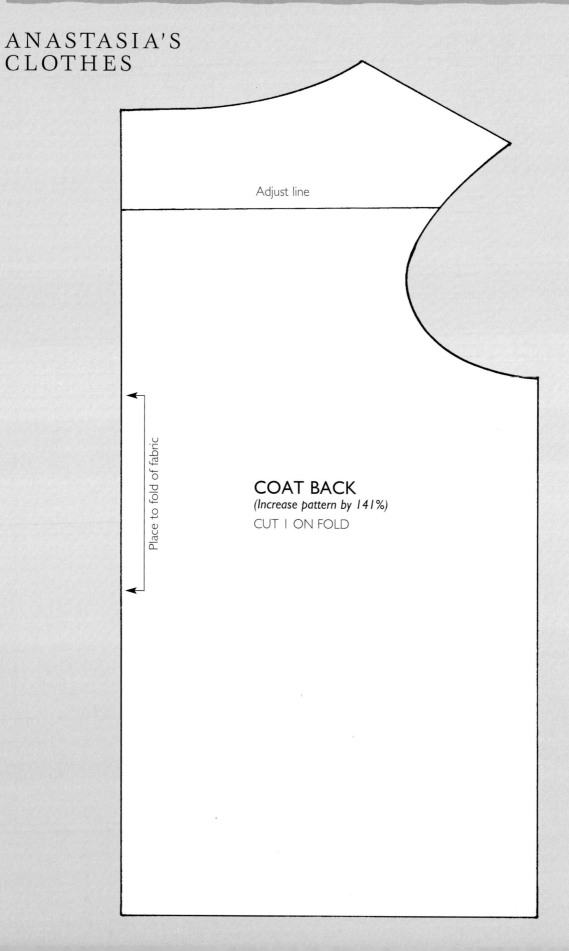

Adjust line

Place to fold of fabric

COAT BACK
(Increase pattern by 141%)
CUT 1 ON FOLD

ANASTASIA'S
CLOTHES

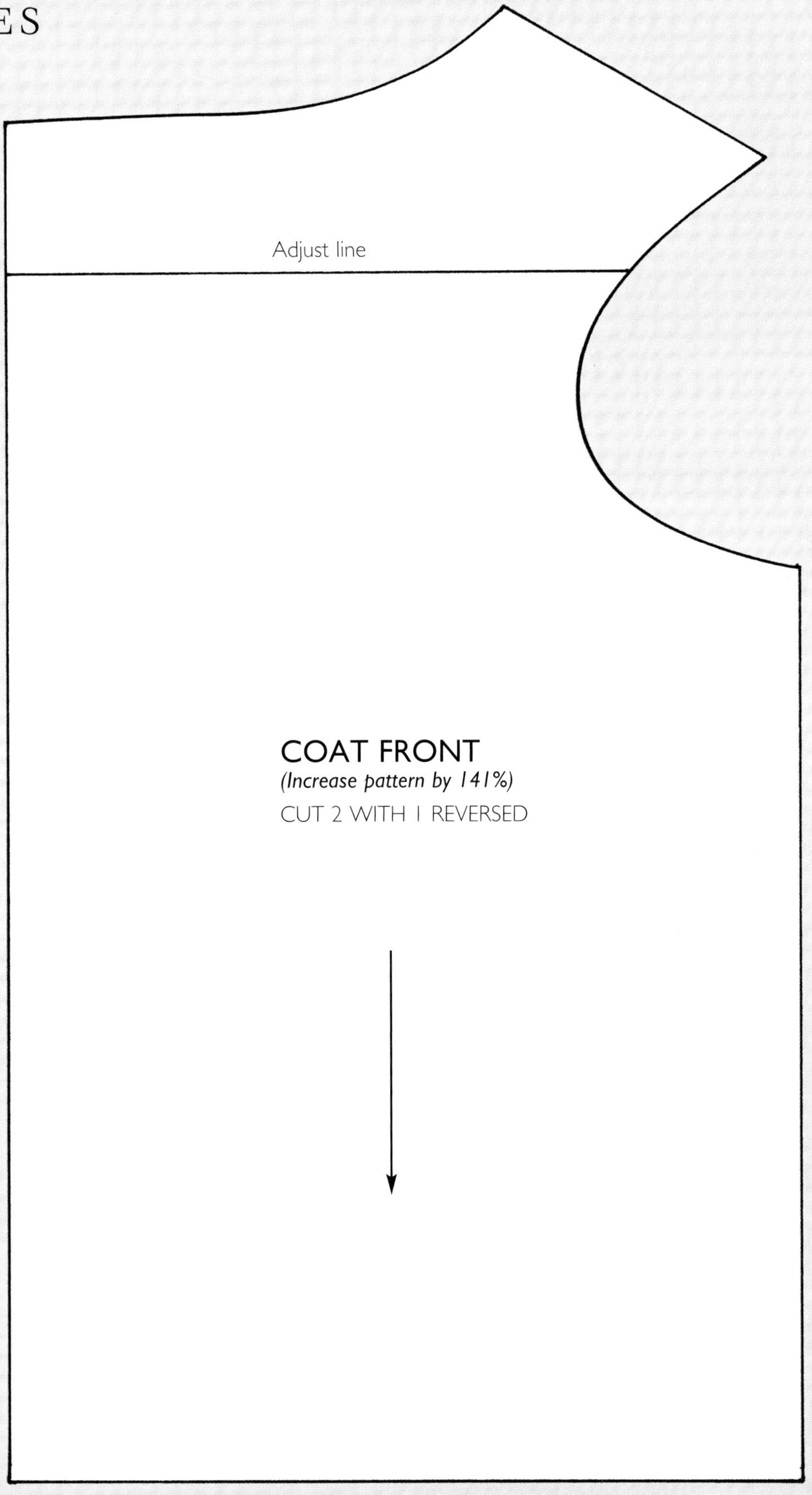

Adjust line

COAT FRONT
(Increase pattern by 141%)
CUT 2 WITH 1 REVERSED

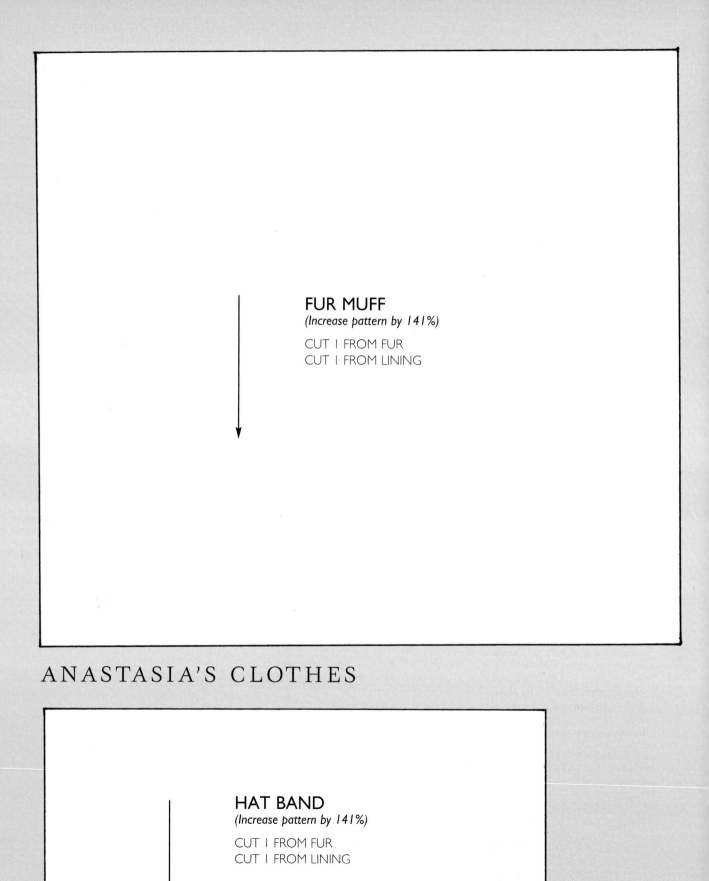

FUR MUFF
(Increase pattern by 141%)

CUT 1 FROM FUR
CUT 1 FROM LINING

ANASTASIA'S CLOTHES

HAT BAND
(Increase pattern by 141%)

CUT 1 FROM FUR
CUT 1 FROM LINING

SUPPLIERS, ACKNOWLEDGEMENTS & FURTHER READING

SUPPLIERS

Further information about teddy bear making materials is available from specialist mail order suppliers. It is advisable to contact the company before requesting catalogues as there is usually a small charge for samples of fabric.

Brian and Donna Gibbs,
Bridon Bears,
Bears Cottage,
42 St Michael's Lane,
Bridport,
Dorset DT6 3RD.
Tel/fax (01308) 420796
Internet web site
http://www.bridonbears.force9.co.uk
Authors of *Making Traditional Teddy Bears* and *Making and Dressing Traditional Teddy Bears*. Designers and suppliers of a large range of traditional and character teddy bear kits, including Georgie (see page 30) in any of the featured colours.

Teddy Bear Warehouse Ltd,
Unit 11, D2 Trading Estate,
Castle Road,
Sittingbourne,
Kent ME10 3RH.
Tel: (01795) 478775
Fax: (01795) 474494
A wide range of English and German mohair fabrics as well as many components and bear-making accessories. Supplied materials for: Poppy, Hugo, Mei Yang; Grandma and Grandpa, as well as various fabrics for the materials section.

Admiral Bears Supplies,
37 Warren Drive,
Ruislip,
Middlesex HA4 9RD.
Tel/fax: 0181-868 9598
A large range of English and German mohair and other bear-making fabrics. Stockists of components, accessories, kits and patterns for teddy bears. Supplied materials for Anastasia and Mei Ying, and fabric for the bear-making step-by-step guide.

Melanie's Little Bear Co.
113 Lodge Road,
Redditch,
Worcestershire B98 7BS.
Tel/fax: (01527) 67575
Mail order supplier for small and miniature bears including a range of fabrics, components and accessories. Kits and patterns for miniature bears are also available. Supplied materials for the 'Bedtime Georgie' miniature teddy bear and fabric and accessories for the materials section.

Edinburgh Imports Inc.
POB 722-Woodland Hills,
California 91365-0722 USA.
Tel: 818 591 3800 Fax: 818 591 3806
Internet web site
http://www.edinburgh.com

Bear Makers' Supplies,
Box 56R Interlochen
MI 49643 USA
Tel (616) 276-7915 Fax (616) 276-7921
Internet web site
http://www.SpareBear.com

OTHER SOURCES

Other international suppliers can be found in various teddy bear magazines and books. Here is a shortlist of those that contain a wealth of information:

Teddy Bear Club International Magazine,
Aceville Publications Ltd,
Castle House,
97 High Street ,
Colchester, CO1 1TH (UK)
Tel (01206) 571322 Fax (01206) 564214
e-mail aceville@globalnet.co.uk

Teddy Bear Times Magazine,
Avalon Court,
Star Road,
Partridge Green,
West Sussex, RH13 8RY (UK)
Tel (01403) 711511 Fax (01403) 711521

Teddy Bear Scene Magazine,
7 Ferringham Lane,
Ferring,
West Sussex BN12 5ND (UK)
Tel (01903) 244900 Fax (01903) 506626

Teddy Bear Review Magazine,
Collector Communications Corp,
170 Fifth Avenue,
New York NY10010 USA
Tel (212) 989-8700

The UK Teddy Bear Guide,
Hugglets PO Box 290,
Brighton BN2 1DR (UK)
Tel (01273) 697974 Fax (01273) 626255
Internet web site
http://www.hugglets.co.uk

ACKNOWLEDGEMENTS

Our very grateful thanks go to: Dave Wikinson of Teddy Bear Warehouse; Jenny Nelson of Admiral Bears Supplies; Melanie Oldnall of Melanie's Little Bear Co for their generous contributions of materials and accessories used throughout this book. Also to Livingstone Textiles Co Ltd (mail order), PO Box 5, St Michael's Lane, Bridport, Dorset DT6 3RS (01308 456844) for most of the clothes fabrics used and for their valuable advice.

Thanks also go to all of the team at David & Charles for their continued support and patience.

Finally, grateful thanks to David Borley and Jennifer Dare of Computer Solutions, 44 St Michael's Lane, Bridport, Dorset DT6 3RD (01308 458541) e-mail computer.solutions@cwcom.net for providing unlimited technical support regarding computer software, hardware and reprographic expertise during the writing of this book…and for being very tolerant neighbours!

INDEX